DOCTRINE OF THE ATONEMENT

William Cunningham

MONERGISM BOOKS

ISBN: 978-1-961807-37-2

CONTENTS

INTRODUCTION

The incarnation of the second person of the Godhead, —the assumption of human nature by One who from eternity had possessed the divine nature, so that He was God and man in one person, —is, as a subject of contemplation, well fitted to call forth the profoundest reverence, and to excite the strongest emotions; and if it was indeed a reality, must have been intended to accomplish most important results. If Christ really was God and man in one person, we may expect to find, in the object thus presented to our contemplation, much that is mysterious— much that we cannot fully comprehend; while we should also be stirred up to examine with the utmost care everything that has been revealed to us regarding it, assured that it must possess no ordinary interest and importance. He who is represented to us in Scripture as being God and man in one person, is also described as the only Mediator between God and man— as the only Saviour of sinners. If it be indeed true, as the Scripture plainly teaches, that the divine and human natures were united in His one person, it is undeniable that this union must have been formed in order to the salvation of sinners, and that the plan which God devised and executed for saving sinners, must just consist in, or be based upon, what Christ, as God and man in one person, did, in order to effect this object. This was the work which the Father gave Him to do; and by doing it He has secured the deliverance from everlasting misery, and the eternal blessedness, of as many as the Father has given Him, —"an innumerable company, which no man can number, out of every kindred, and nation, and people, and tongue."

CHAPTER ONE

CONNECTION BETWEEN THE PERSON AND WORK OF CHRIST

I n systematic expositions of the scheme of divine truth, the subject of the person of the Mediator, or the scriptural account of who and what Christ was, is usually followed by the subject of the work of Christ, or the account of what he did for the salvation of sinners. The terms commonly employed by theologians to describe in general the work of Christ as Mediator, are munus and officium; and divines of almost all classes have admitted, that the leading features of the scriptural representations of what Christ did for the salvation of sinners, might be fully brought out, by ascribing to Him the three offices of a Prophet, a

Priest, and a King, and by unfolding what it was he did in the execution of these three offices.

It is plain, from the nature of the case, that the subjects of the person and the work of Christ must be, in fact and in doctrine, intimately connected with each other. If the Mediator was God and man in one person, then we might confidently expect that He would do, and that it would be necessary for Him to do, in order to the salvation of sinners, what no man, what no creature, was competent to do. And when we survey what Scripture seems to hold up to us as the work which He wrought for our salvation, we can scarcely fail to be impressed with the conviction, that, from its very nature, it required one who was possessed of infinite perfection and excellence to accomplish it. Accordingly, we find that the admission or denial of Christ's divinity has always affected fundamentally the whole of men's views in regard to almost everything in the scheme of salvation, and especially in regard to Christ's mediatorial work.

Socinians, holding that Christ was a mere man, teach, in perfect consistency with this, that He did nothing for the salvation of men except what may be comprehended under the general head or description of revealing, confirming, and illustrating truth or doctrine, and of setting us an example, —a work to which any creature, even a mere man, of course employed and qualified by God for the purpose, was perfectly competent. Arians, —holding Christ to be a superhuman, but still a created, and not a divine or infinite being, —are accustomed, in accordance with this view of the person of the Mediator, to introduce an additional and somewhat higher notion into their representation of the nature of His work. It is, in substance, that of influence exerted by Him with God, in order to prevail upon Him to pardon sinners and admit them into the enjoyment of His favour. Christ, as a highly exalted creature, who took a deep interest in the salvation of sinners, and was willing to endure, and did endure, humiliation and suffering on their account, did what was very meritorious in itself and very acceptable to God; and thus acquired such influence with God, as that He consented, at Christ's request, and from a regard to Him, and to what he had done, to forgive sinners, and to bestow upon them spiritual blessings. This is, in substance, the view entertained of the general nature of Christ's work by those who regard Him as an exalted, superangelic creature; and I fear that a vague impression of something similar to this, and not going much beyond it, floats in the minds of many amongst us, who have never thought or speculated on religious subjects. Almost all who have held the doctrine of Christ's proper divinity, have also believed that His sufferings and death were vicarious, —that is, that they were endured in the room and stead of sinners, —and have regarded the most important, peculiar, and essential features of His mediatorial work to be His substitution in our room and stead, —the satisfaction which He rendered to divine justice, —though it must be admitted, that there have been differences of opinion, of no small importance, among those who have concurred in maintaining these general scriptural truths with respect both to the person and the work of Christ.

It is one of the peculiar features of the theology of the present day, that this remarkable and important connection of great principles is overlooked or denied. There are many in the present day, who make a profession of believing in the proper divinity, and even in the eternal Sonship, of the Saviour, who yet deny the doctrine that has been general- ly held in the Christian church concerning the atonement, and put forth, upon this point, notions substantially the same as those of the Socinians and Arians. They give prominence to the mere incarnation of Christ, without connecting and combining it with His sufferings and death, and with His fulfilment of all righteousness in their room and stead, resolving it into a mere manifestation of the divine character and purposes, intended to make an impression upon our minds. But they have not succeeded in bringing out anything like an adequate cause for so remarkable a peculiarity as the assumption of human nature by the second person of the Godhead; while a confirmation of the great principles we have laid down about the connection of doctrine is to be found in the fact, that the views of these men, even about the divinity of the Son, however plausibly they may sometimes be put forth, turn out, when carefully examined, to be materially different from those which have been usually held in the Christian church, as taught in Scripture; and resolve very much into a kind of Platonic Sabellianism, which explains-away any really personal distinction in the Godhead, and thus becomes virtually identified with the ordinary view of Socinians or Unitarians. The fact that influential writers in the present day make a profession of believing in the divinity and incarnation of the Saviour, while denying His vicarious and satisfactory atonement, is a reason why we should make it an object to understand and develop fully the connection between these two great departments of scriptural truth; to perceive and to explain, —so far as Scripture affords any materials for doing so, —how the one leads to and supports the other, —how the incarnation and atonement of our Lord are closely and indissolubly connected together, —and how, in combination, they form the ground and basis of all our hopes.

There is a manifest enough congruity between the three distinctive schemes of doctrine, as to the person of the Mediator, and the corresponding opinions with respect to His work; and there would, of course, be nothing strange in this, if the whole subject were one of mere intellectual speculation, in regard to which men were warranted and called upon to follow out their own views to all their legitimate logical results. But since all parties profess to derive their views upon this subject from the statements of Scripture, exactly and critically interpreted, it is somewhat singular that they should all find in Scripture a line of different opinions in regard to Christ's work running parallel to a corresponding series in regard to His person. The fact affords too good reasons for the conclusion, that it is very common for men, even when professing to be simply investigating the meaning of scriptural statements, to be greatly, if not chiefly, influenced by certain previous notions of a general kind, which, whether upon good grounds or not, they have been led to form, as to what Scripture does say, or should say; and is thus fitted to impress upon us the important lesson, that if we would escape the guilt of distorting and perverting the whole word of God, and of misunderstanding the whole scheme of salvation, we must be very careful to derive all our views, upon matters of religious doctrine, from the sacred Scripture, in place of getting them from some other source, and then bringing them to it, and virtually employing them, more or less openly and palpably, to overrule its authority, and to pervert its meaning.

I have said that it has been the general practice of theologians since the Reformation, to expound the scriptural doctrine concerning the work of Christ as Mediator, in the way of ascribing to Him the three distinct offices of a Prophet, a Priest, and a King; and then classifying and illustrating, under these three heads, the different departments of the work which He wrought for the salvation of sinners. This division, if represented and applied as one which certainly comprehends and exhausts the subject, cannot be said to have direct scriptural authority; and yet there is enough in Scripture to suggest and warrant the adoption of it, as a useful and convenient arrangement, though nothing to warrant us in drawing inferences or conclusions from it, as if it were both accurate and complete. The ground or warrant for it is this: —that it is very easy to prove from Scripture that Christ, as Mediator, is a Prophet, a Priest, and a King; that He executed the functions of these three different offices; and that all the leading departments of His work, —of what He did for the salvation of sinners, as it is set before us in Scripture, —fall naturally and easily under the ordinary and appropriate functions of these different offices. The propriety and utility of this division have been a good deal discussed by some continental writers. Ernesti— who was, however, much more eminent as a critic than as a theologian— laboured to show, in a dissertation, "De officio Christi triplici," published in his Opuscula Theologica, that the division has no sanction from Scripture, and is fitted only to introduce confusion and error; and his views and arguments have been adopted by Doederlein, Morus, and Knapp, There is, however, very little force in their objections, and the division continues still to be generally adopted by the most eminent continental theologians of the present clay. The leading point which the opponents of this division labour to establish is, that in Scripture the functions of these different offices are not always exactly discriminated from each other. But this position, even though proved, is very little to the purpose: for it can scarcely be disputed that Scripture docs afford us sufficient materials for forming pretty definite conceptions of the respective natures and functions of these three offices, as distinct from each other; and that, in point of fact, the leading departments of Christ's work admit easily and naturally of being classed under the heads of the appropriate functions of these three offices, as the Scripture ordinarily discriminates them. This is quite sufficient to sanction the distinction as unobjectionable, useful, and convenient; while, of course, as it proves nothing of itself, all must admit the obligation lying upon those who make use of it to produce distinct and satisfactory scriptural proof of every position they maintain, as to the nature, object, and effects of anything that Christ is alleged to have done in the execution of these different offices.

It may be described in general, as the characteristic of the Socinian system of theology upon this subject, that it regards Christ merely as a Prophet, —that is, merely as revealing and establishing truths or doctrines concerning God and divine things, —while it denies that He executed the office of a Priest or of a King. But while this is true in substance there are one or two explanations that may assist us in understanding the discussions which occur upon this subject among the older theologians. The original Socinians, as I have already had occasion to mention, usually admitted that Christ executed the office of a King, and they did not altogether, and in every sense, deny that he executed the office of a Priest; while they conjoined or confounded the priestly and the kingly offices. I then explained, that though very far from being deficient either in ingenuity or in courage, they were unable to evade the evidence that Christ, after His resurrection, was raised to a station of exalted power, which in some way or other he employed for promoting the spiritual and eternal welfare of men. Their leading position, in regard to Christ's priestly office, was, that he did not execute it at all upon earth, but only after His ascension to heaven; and that, of course, His sufferings and death formed no part of it, —these being intended merely to afford us an example of virtue, and to confirm and establish the doctrine of the immortality of the soul. The execution of His priestly office did not commence till after His ascension, and was only an aspect or modification of the kingly office, or of the exercise of the powers with which He had been invested; while everything connected with the objects to which this power was directed, or the way and manner in which it was exercised, was left wholly unexplained. Modern Socinians, having discovered that Scripture gives us no definite information as to the place which Christ now occupies,

and the manner in which he is now engaged; and being satisfied that all
that is said in Scripture about His priesthood is wholly figurative, —and,
moreover, that the figure means nothing, real or true, being taken from
mere Jewish notions, —have altogether discarded both the priestly and
the kingly offices, and have thus brought out somewhat more plainly and
openly, what the old Socinians held in substance, though they conveyed
it in a more scriptural phraseology.

It is under the head of the priestly office of Christ that the great and infinitely important subject of His satisfaction or atonement is discussed;
and this may be regarded as the most peculiar and essential feature of the
work which he wrought, as Mediator, for the salvation of sinners, —that
which stands in most immediate and necessary connection with the
divinity of His person. We can conceive it possible that God might have
given us a very full revelation of His will, and abundantly confirmed the
certainty of the information which He communicated, as well as have set
before us a complete pattern of every virtue for our imitation, through
the instrumentality of a creature, or even of a mere man. We can conceive
a creature exalted by God to a very high pitch of power and dignity, and
made the instrument, in the exercise of this power, of accomplishing very
important results bearing upon the spiritual and eternal welfare of men.
But when the ideas of satisfying the divine justice and the divine law, in
the room and stead of sinners, —and thereby reconciling men to God,
whose law they had broken, —are presented to our minds, and in some
measure realized, here we cannot but be impressed with the conviction,
that if these ideas describe actual realities, we have got into a region in
which there is no scope for the agency or operation of a mere creature,
and in which infinite power and perfection are called for. We are not,
indeed, to imagine that we fully and rightly understand the prophetical
office of the Mediator, unless we regard the great Revealer of God as one

who was the brightness of His glory and the express image of His person, —as having been from eternity in the bosom of the Father. And it is proper also to remember, that we can scarcely conceive it to be possible that the actual power and dominion which the Scriptures ascribe to Christ as Mediator, and which II(;s ever exercising in the execution of His kingly office, —including, as it does, the entire government of the universe, and the absolute disposal of the everlasting destinies of all men, —could be delegated to, and exercised by, any creature, however exalted. We only wish to remark, that the general ideas of revealing God's will, and exercising power or dominion, —which may be said to constitute the essence of the doctrine concerning the prophetical and kingly offices of Christ, —are more within the range of our ordinary conceptions; and that though, in point of fact, applicable to Christ in a way in which they could not apply to any creature, yet they do not of themselves suggest so readily the idea of the necessity of a divine Mediator as those which are commonly associated with the priestly office. The priestly office, accordingly, has been the principal subject of controversial discussion, both from its more immediate connection with the proper divinity of Christ's person, and from its more extensive and influential bearing upon all the provisions and arrangements of the scheme of salvation.

It is very manifest, on the most cursory survey of the sacred Scriptures, that the salvation of sinners is ascribed to the sufferings and death of Christ, —that His sufferings and death are represented as intimately connected with, and influentially bearing upon, this infinitely important result. Indeed, the whole subject which is now under consideration may be regarded, in one aspect of it, as virtually resolving into the investigation of this question, —What is the relation subsisting between the sufferings and death of Christ and the salvation of sinners'? In what precise way do they bear upon men's obtaining or receiving the forgiveness of their sins and the enjoyment of God's favour? And in further considering this subject, it will be convenient, for the sake both of distinctness and brevity, to advert only to the death of Christ; for though most of the advocates of the generally received doctrine of the atonement regard the whole of Christ's humiliation and sufferings, from His incarnation to His crucifixion, as invested with a priestly, sacrificial, and piacular character, —as constituting His once offering up of Himself a sacrifice, —as all propitiatory of God, and expiatory of men's sins, —yet, in accordance with the general representations of Scripture, they regard His oblation or sacrifice of Himself, as a piacular victim, as principally manifested, and as concentrated in His pouring out His soul unto death, —His bearing our sins in His own body on the tree. And we may also, for the same reasons, —and because we do not intend at present to discuss the whole subject of justification, and the bearing of Christ's work upon all that is implied in that word, —speak generally, and in the first instance, in adverting to the object to be effected, of the pardon or forgiveness of men's sins, —an expression sometimes used in Scripture as virtually including or implying the whole of our salvation, because it is a fundamental part of it, and because it may be justly regarded as, in some respects, the primary thing to be attended to in considering our relation to God and our everlasting destinies.

We have already stated generally the different doctrines or theories which have been propounded, —all professing to rest upon scriptural authority, —in regard to the connection between the death of Christ and the forgiveness of men's sins, taking these two expressions in the sense now explained. The Socinian doctrine is, that the death of Christ bears upon this result merely by confirming and illustrating truths, and by setting an example of virtue; and thus affording motives and encouragements to the exercise of repentance and the performance of good actions, by which we ourselves procure or obtain for ourselves the forgiveness of sin and the enjoyment of God's favour, —its whole power and efficacy being thus placed in the confirmation of truth and in the exhibition of exemplary virtue. The doctrine commonly held by Arians is, that Christ, by submitting to suffering and to death, on men's account, and with a view to their benefit, has done what was very acceptable to God, and has thus obtained a position of influence with God, which He exercises by interceding in some way or other for the purpose of procuring for men forgiveness and favour. Now, it may be said to be true, that the Scripture does ascribe these effects to the death of Christ, and that, of course, that event is fitted, and was intended, to produce them. The death of Christ was a testimony to truths, and is well adapted to establish and illustrate them, though what these truths are must depend essentially upon what that event was in its whole character and bearing.

It is fitted, and of course was intended, to afford us motives and encouragements to repentance and holiness. This is true, but it is very far from being the whole of the truth upon the subject. It is likewise true that Scripture sanctions the general idea of Christ— by suffering and dying for the sake of men— doing what was pleasing and acceptable to God, —of His being in consequence rewarded, and raised to a position of high power and dignity, —and of His interceding with God, or using influence with Him, to procure for men spiritual blessings. All this is true, and it is held by those who maintain the commonly received doctrine of the atonement. But neither is this the whole of the truth which Scripture teaches upon the subject. And what in it is true, as ' thus generally expressed, is not brought out so fully and explicitly, as the Scripture affords us ample materials for doing, by connecting it with the doctrine of the atonement.

Some men would fain persuade us that the substance of all that Scripture teaches us concerning the way of salvation is this, —that an exalted and glorious Being interposed on behalf of sinners, —mediated between them and an offended God; and by this interposition and influence procured for them the forgiveness of their sins, and the enjoyment of God's favour. Now, all this is true. There is nothing in this general statement which contradicts or opposes anything that is taught us in Scripture. But, just as the Scripture affords us, as we have seen, abundant materials for defining much more fully and explicitly the real nature, dignity, and position of this exalted Being, and leaves us not to mere vague generalities upon this point, but warrants and requires us to believe and maintain that He was of the same nature and substance with the Father, and equal in power and glory; so, in like manner, in regard to what He did for men's salvation, the Scripture does not leave us to the vague generalities of His mediating or interposing, interceding or using influence, on our behalf, but affords us abundant materials for explaining much more precisely and definitely the nature or kind of His mediation or interposition, —the foundation of His intercession, —the ground or source of His influence. The commonly received doctrine of the satisfaction or atonement of Christ just professes to bring out this more full and specific information; and the substance of it is this, —that the way and manner in which He mediated or interposed in behalf of sinners, and in order to effect their deliverance or salvation, was by putting Himself in their place, —by substituting Himself in their room and stead, —suffering, as their substitute or surety, the penalty of the law which they had broken, the punishment which they had deserved by their sins, —and thereby satisfying the claims of divine justice, and thus reconciling them to God. This great scriptural doctrine is thus expressed in our Confession of Faith: "The Lord Jesus, by His perfect

obedience and sacrifice of Himself, which He through the eternal Spirit
once offered up unto God, hath fully satisfied the justice of His Father;
and purchased not only reconciliation, but an everlasting inheritance
in the kingdom of heaven, for all those whom the Father hath given
unto Him;" or, in the words of the Shorter Catechism, "Christ executeth
the office of a Priest, in His once offering up of Himself a sacrifice to
satisfy divine justice, and reconcile us to God; and in making continual
intercession for us."

Here I may remark, as illustrating some preceding observations,
—though this is not a topic which I mean to dwell upon, —that His
intercession succeeds, and is based upon, His sacrifice and satisfaction;
and that thus distinctness and definiteness are given to the idea which
it expresses. When men's deliverance, or their possession of spiritual
blessings, is ascribed, in general, to the intercession of Christ, without
being accompanied with an exposition of His vicarious sacrifice and
satisfaction, as the ground or basis on which it rests, no more definite
meaning can be attached to it than merely that of rising some influence,
in order to procure for men what they need from God. But when His
vicarious sacrifice and satisfaction are first asserted as the great leading
department of the work which He wrought for the salvation of sinners,
and His intercession is then introduced as following this, and based upon
it, we escape from this vague generality, and are warranted and enabled to
represent His intercession as implying that He pleads with God, in behalf
of men, and in order to obtain for them the forgiveness of their sins, this
most relevant and weighty consideration, —viz., that he has suffered in
their room, that He has endured in their stead the whole penalty which
their sins had deserved.

The great doctrine, that Christ offered Himself as a vicarious sacrifice,
—that is, a sacrifice in the room and stead of sinners, as their surety

and substitute; that He did so, in order to satisfy divine justice and reconcile them to God; and that, of course, by doing so, He has satisfied divine justice and reconciled them to God, —has been always held and maintained by the great body of the Christian church. It was not, indeed, like the doctrines of the Trinity and the person of Christ, subjected, at an early period in the history of the church, to a thorough and searching controversial discussion; and, in consequence of this, men's views in regard to it continued always to partake somewhat of the character of vagueness and indistinctness. It can scarcely be said to have been fully expounded and discussed, in such a way as to bring out thoroughly its true nature and its scriptural grounds, until after the publication of the works of Socinus; for Anselm's contributions to the right exposition of this doctrine, important as they are, scarcely come up to this description. It formed no part of the controversy between the Reformers and the Romanists; for the Church of Rome has always continued to profess the substance of scriptural truth on this subject, as well as on that of the Trinity, though, according to her usual practice, she has grievously corrupted, and almost wholly neutralized, the truth which she professedly holds. Socinus was the first who made a full and elaborate effort to overturn the doctrine which the church had always held upon this subject, and which, though not very fully or explicitly developed as a topic of speculation, had constituted the source at once of the hopes and the motives of God's people from the beginning. This he did chiefly in his Treatise, "De Jesu Christo Servatore," and in his "Pralectiones Theologicae;" and it certainly required no ordinary ingenuity for one man, and without the benefit of much previous discussion upon the point, to devise a whole system of plausible evasions and perversions, for the purpose of showing that the doctrine which the whole church had hitherto believed upon the subject was not taught in Scripture. Ever

since that period the doctrine of the atonement or satisfaction of Christ
has been very fully discussed in all its bearings and aspects, affecting as it
does, and must do, the whole scheme of Christian truth; and the result
has been, that the Socinian evasions and perversions of Scripture have
been triumphantly exposed, and that the generally received doctrine of
the church has been conclusively established, and placed upon an im-
movable basis, by the most exact and searching investigation, conducted
upon the soundest and strictest critical principles, into the meaning
of the numerous and varied scriptural statements that bear upon this
subject.

In considering this subject, I propose to advert, in the first place, to
the doctrine of the atonement or satisfaction of Christ in general, as
held by the universal church, —by Papists, Lutherans, Calvinists, and
Arminians, —in opposition to the Socinians and other deniers of our
Lord's divinity; in the second place, to the peculiarities of the Arminian
doctrine upon this subject, as affected and determined by its relation to
the general system of Arminian theology; and in the third place, to the
doctrine which has been propounded, upon this subject, by those who
profess Calvinistic principles upon other points, but who, upon this,
hold views identical with, or closely resembling those of, the Arminians,
especially in regard to the extent of the atonement.

CHAPTER TWO

NECESSITY OF THE ATONEMENT

I n considering the subject of the atonement, it may be proper to advert, in the first place, to a topic which has given rise to a good deal of discussion, —namely, the necessity of an atonement or satisfaction, in order to the forgiveness of men's sins. The Socinians allege that a vicarious atonement or satisfaction for sin is altogether unnecessary, and adduce this consideration as a proof, or at least a presumption, against its truth or reality; while the advocates of an atonement have not been contented with showing that its non-necessity could not be proved, but have, in general, further averred positively that it was necessary, —have undertaken to prove this, —and have made the evidence of its necessity at once an argument in favour of its truth and reality, and a means of illustrating its real nature and operation. The assertion, as well as the denial, of the necessity of an atonement, must, from the nature of the case, be based upon certain ideas of the attributes and moral government of God, viewed in connection with the actual state and condition of man as a transgressor of His law; and the subject thus leads to discussions in which there is a great danger of indulging in presumptuous speculations on points of which we can know nothing, except in so far as God has been pleased to convey to us information in His word. It can scarcely be said that the Scripture gives us any direct or explicit information upon the precise question, whether or not the salvation of sinners could possibly have been effected in any other way than through an atonement or satisfaction; and it is not indispensable for any important purpose that this question should be determined. The only point of vital importance is that of the truth or reality of an atonement, and then the consideration of its true nature and bearing. We have just to ascertain from Scripture what was the true character and object of Christ's death, and the way and manner in which, in point of fact, it bears upon the forgiveness of men's sins, and their relation to God and to His law; and when we have ascertained this, it cannot be of fundamental importance that we should investigate and determine the question, whether or not it was possible for God to have forgiven men without satisfaction.

Had the materials for determining the question of the truth and reality of an atonement been scanty or obscure, then the presumption arising from anything we might be able to know or ascertain as to its necessity or non-necessity, might be of some avail in turning the scale upon the question of its truth or reality. But when we have in Scripture such explicit and abundant materials for establishing the great doctrine that, in point of fact, Christ did offer up Himself a sacrifice to satisfy divine justice, we are entitled to feel, and we ought to feel, that, in stating and arguing this question, we are wholly independent of the alleged necessity or non-necessity of an atonement; and having ascertained what God has done, —what provision He has made, —what scheme He has adopted, —we need not be very anxious about settling the question, whether or not He could have accomplished the result in any other way or by any other means. But while it is proper that we should understand that this question about the necessity of an atonement is not one of vital importance in defending our cause against the Socinians, as we have full and abundant evidence of its truth and reality; yet, since the subject has been largely discussed among theologians, —since almost all who have held the truth and reality of an atonement have also maintained its necessity, —and since the consideration of the subject brings out some views which, though not indispensable to the proof of its truth or reality, are yet true and important in themselves, and very useful in illustrating its nature and bearings, —it may be proper to give a brief notice of the points that are usually introduced into the discussion of this question.

Let us first advert to the ground taken by the Socinians upon this department of the subject. They deny the necessity of an atonement or satisfaction for sin, upon the ground that the essential benevolence and compassion of God must have prompted, and that His supreme dominion must have enabled, Him to forgive men's sins without any atonement or satisfaction; and that there was nothing in His nature, government, or law, which threw any obstacle in the way of His at once exercising His sovereign dominion in accordance with the promptings of His compassion, and extending forgiveness to all upon the condition of repentance and reformation.

Now, in the first place, an allegation of this sort is sufficiently met by the scriptural proof, that, in point of fact, an atonement was offered, —that satisfaction was made, and that forgiveness and salvation are held out to men, and bestowed upon them, only on the footing of this atonement. And then, in the second place, if we should, ex abundanti, examine the Socinian position more directly, it is no difficult matter to show that they have not proved, and cannot prove, any one of the positions on which they rest the alleged non-necessity of an atonement. As they commonly allege that the doctrine of the Trinity is a denial of the divine unity, so they usually maintain that the doctrine of the atonement involves a denial of the divine placability. That placability is an attribute or quality of God, is unquestionable. This general position can be fully established from revelation, however doubtful or uncertain may be the proof of it derived from reason or nature. Independently altogether of general scriptural declarations, it is established by the facts, that, as all admit, God desired and determined to forgive and to save sinners who had broken His law, and made provision for carrying this gracious purpose into effect. But there is no particular statement in Scripture, and no general principle clearly sanctioned by it, which warrants us to assert that God's placability required of Him that He should forgive men's sins without an atonement, and upon the mere condition of repentance. Placability is not the only attribute or quality of God. There are other features of His character, established both by His works and His word, which, viewed by themselves, are manifestly fitted to lead us to draw an opposite conclusion as to the way in which he would, in point of fact, deal with sin and sinners, —well fitted to excite the apprehension that he will inflict upon them the punishment which, by their sins, they have merited. In these circumstances, it is utterly unwarrantable for us, without clear authority from Scripture, to indulge in dogmatic assertions as to what God certainly will, or will not, do in certain circumstances.

Neither Scripture nor reason warrant the position that repentance is, in its own nature, an adequate reason or ground, ordinarily and in general, and still less in all cases, for pardoning those who have transgressed a law to which they were subject. It is in entire accordance with the dictates of reason, and with the ordinary practice of men, to inflict the full penalty of the law upon repentant criminals; and there is no ground on which we are warranted to assert that God cannot, or certainly will not, follow a similar course in regard to those who have transgressed His law.

The Socinians are accustomed, in discussing this point, to dwell upon the scriptural statements with respect to repentance, its necessity and importance, and the connection subsisting between it and forgiveness. But there is nothing in these statements which establishes the position they undertake to maintain upon this subject. Those statements prove, indeed, that sinners are under an imperative obligation to repent; and they prove further, that, according to the arrangements which God has actually made, an invariable connection subsists between forgiveness and repentance, so that it is true that without repentance there is no forgiveness, and that wherever there is real repentance, forgiveness is bestowed; and that thus men are commanded and bound to repent in order to their being forgiven, and are warranted to infer their forgiveness from their repentance. The scriptural statements prove all this, but they prove nothing more; and this is not enough to give support to the Socinian argument. All this may be true, while it may still be false that repentance is the sole cause or condition of the forgiveness, —the sole, or even the principal, reason on account of which it is bestowed; and if so, then there is abundant room left for the admission of the principle, that a vicarious atonement or satisfaction was also necessary in order to the forgiveness of sin, and was indeed the true ground on which the forgiveness was conferred.

But while it is thus shown that this may be true, in entire consistency with all that Scripture says about forgiveness, and the connection between it and repentance, and while this is amply sufficient to refute the Socinian argument; we undertake further to prove from Scripture, that the atonement or satisfaction of Christ is indeed the ground on which forgiveness rests, and that this principle must be taken in, and must have its proper place assigned to it, if we would receive and maintain the whole doctrine which the word of God plainly teaches us in regard to this most momentous subject. But, more than this, the advocates of the generally received doctrine of the atonement not only deny and disprove the Socinian allegation of its non-necessity, —not only show that Socinians cannot prove that it was not necessary, —they themselves, in general, positively aver that it was necessary, and think they can produce satisfactory evidence of the truth of this position. There is, at first view, something repulsive— as having the appearance of unwarranted presumption— in asserting the necessity of an atonement or satisfaction, as it really amounts in substance to this, that God could not have pardoned men unless an atonement had been made, —unless a satisfaction had been rendered for their sins; and it may appear more suited to the modesty and reverence with which we ought to speak on such a subject, to say, that, for aught we know, God might have saved men in other ways, or through other means, but that he has adopted that method or scheme which was the wisest and the best, —best fitted to promote His own glory, and secure the great ends of His moral government. We find, however, upon further consideration, that the case is altogether so peculiar, and that the grounds of the assertion are so clear and strong, as to warrant it, even though an explicit deliverance upon this precise point is not given us in Scripture.

As to the general position, that an atonement or satisfaction was necessary, —or rather, that God could not have made provision for pardoning and saving sinners in any other way than that which he has actually adopted, —this seems fully warranted, independently of any other consideration, by the Scripture doctrine of the proper divinity of the Saviour. The incarnation of the eternal Son of God, —the assumption of human nature by One who was at the same time possessor of the divine, —the fact that this Being, who is God and man in one person, spent a life on earth of obscurity and humiliation, —that he endured many sufferings and indignities, and was at last subjected to a cruel and ignominious death; — all this, if it be true, —if it be an actual reality, —as Scripture requires us to believe, is so peculiar and extraordinary in its whole character and aspects, that whenever we are led to realize it, we feel ourselves at once irresistibly constrained to say, that this would not have taken place if it had been possible that the result to which it was directed, —namely, the forgiveness and salvation of sinners, —could have been effected in any other way, or by any other means. We feel, and we cannot but feel, that there is no unwarranted presumption in saying, that if it had been possible that the salvation of guilty men could have been otherwise accomplished, the only-begotten Son of God would not have left the glory which He had with His Father from eternity, assumed human nature, and suffered and died on earth. This ground, were there nothing more revealed regarding it, would warrant us to make the general assertion, that the incarnation, suffering, and death of Christ were necessary to the salvation of sinners, —that this result could not have been effected without them. This consideration, indeed, has no weight with Socinians, as they do not admit the grand peculiarity on which it is based, —namely, the divinity and the incarnation of Him who came to save sinners. Still it is an ample warrant for our general assertion, as being clearly implied in, and certainly deducible from, a doctrine which we undertake to prove to be plainly revealed in Scripture.

It ought, however, to be noticed, that the precise position which this general consideration warrants us to assert, is not directly and immediately the necessity of an atonement or satisfaction, but only the necessity of the sufferings and death of Christ, whatever may have been the character attaching to them, or the precise effect immediately resulting from them, in connection with the salvation of sinners; and that, accordingly, it was only the warrantableness of introducing the idea, and the expression of necessity, as applicable to the subject in general, that we had in view in bringing it forward; and we have now to advert to the indications supposed to be given us in Scripture, of the grounds or reasons of this necessity. Scripture fully warrants us in saying that there are things which God cannot do. It says expressly that he cannot deny Himself; that he cannot he; that he cannot repent (though there is an improper sense in which repentance is ascribed to Him); and he cannot do these things, just because He is God, and not man, —because He is possessed of divine and infinite perfection. And if it be in any sense true that an atonement or satisfaction was necessary, —or, what is in substance the same thing, that God could not have pardoned sinners without it, —this must be because the attributes of His nature, or the principles of His government, —in other words, His excellence or perfection, —prevented or opposed it, or threw obstacles in the way, which could not otherwise be removed. Accordingly, this is the general position which the advocates of the necessity of an atonement maintain.

The most obvious and palpable consideration usually adduced in support of the necessity of an atonement, is that derived from the law of God, especially the threatenings which, in the law, he has denounced against transgressors. The law which God has promulgated is this, "The soul which sinneth shall die." If God has indeed said this, —if he has uttered this threatening, —this would seem to render it certain and necessary, that wherever sin has been committed, death, with all that it includes or implies, should be inflicted, unless God were to repent, or to deny Himself, or to be, —all which the Scripture assures us He cannot do, because of the perfection of His nature. And it is a remarkable coincidence, that the only cases in which Scripture says explicitly that God cannot do certain things, all bear upon and confirm the position, that he cannot pardon sin without an atonement; inasmuch as to say, that he could pardon sin without an atonement, would, in the circumstances, amount to a virtual declaration that He could he, that He could repent, that He could deny Himself. Upon this ground, the possibility of men who had sinned escaping death, —that is, everlasting misery, —would seem to be precluded. If such a being as God is has threatened sin with the punishment of death, there must be a serious difficulty in the way of sinners escaping. His veracity seems to prevent this, and to present an insuperable obstacle. In pardoning sinners, or in exempting them from the death which they have incurred, it would seem that He must trample upon His own law, and disregard His own threatening; and this the very perfection of His nature manifestly forbids.

Socinians, indeed, have been accustomed to allege, that though God is obliged by His veracity to perform His promises, —because by promising He has conferred upon His creatures a right to the fulfilment of the promise, —yet that His veracity does not oblige Him to fulfil His threatenings, because the party to whose case they apply has no right, and puts forth no claim, to their infliction. But this is a mere evasion of the difficulty. God is a law unto Himself. His own inherent perfection obliges Him always to do what is right and just, and that irrespective of any rights which His creatures may have acquired, or any claims which they may prefer. On this ground, His veracity seems equally to require that He should execute threatenings, as that He should fulfil promises. If He does not owe this to sinners, He owes it to Himself. When he threatened sin with the punishment of death, He was not merely giving an abstract declaration as to what sin merited, and might justly bring upon those who committed it; He was declaring the way and manner in which He would, in fact, treat it when it occurred. The law denouncing death as the punishment of sin was thus a virtual prediction of what

God would do in certain circumstances; and when these circumstances occurred, His veracity required that he should act as He had foretold.

We can conceive of no way in which it is possible that the honour and integrity of the divine law could be maintained, or the divine veracity be preserved pure and unstained, if sinners were not subjected to death, except by an adequate atonement or satisfaction being rendered in their room and stead. No depth of reflection, no extent of experience, could suggest anything but this, which could render the sinner's exemption from death possible. There is much in the history of the world to suggest this, but nothing whatever to suggest anything else. We are not entitled, indeed, apart from the discoveries of revelation, to assert that even this would render the pardon of the sinner possible, consistently with the full exercise of the divine veracity, and full maintenance of the honour of the divine law; and still less are we entitled to assert that, even if an adequate atonement or satisfaction might render the escape of the sinner possible, it was further possible that such an atonement or satisfaction could in fact be rendered. We are not warranted to assert these things independently of revelation; but we have strong grounds for asserting that, if God did threaten death as the punishment of sin, nothing could have prevented the infliction of the threatening, and rendered the escape of the sinner possible, except an adequate atonement or satisfaction, —that this at least was indispensable, if even this could have been of any avail.

But those who hold the necessity of an atonement or satisfaction in order to the pardon of the sin, and the escape of the sinner, usually rest it, not merely upon the law of God as revealed, and upon His veracity as concerned in the execution of the threatenings which He has publicly denounced, but also upon the inherent perfection of His nature, independently of any declaration He may have made, or any prediction He may have uttered, —and more especially upon His justice. The discussion of this point leads us into some more abstruse and difficult inquiries than the former; and it must be confessed that here we have not such clear and certain materials for our conclusions, and that we should feel deeply the necessity of following closely the guidance and direction of Scripture. The representations given us in Scripture of the justice of God, are fitted to impress upon us the conviction that it requires Him to give to every one his due, —what he has merited by his conduct, —and, of course, to give to the sinner the punishment which he has deserved. What God has threatened, His veracity requires Him to inflict, because He has threatened it. But the threatening itself must have originated in the inherent perfection of His own nature prompting Him to punish sin as it deserves; and to threaten to punish, because it is already and antecedently right to do so. God's law, or His revealed will, declaring what His creatures should do, and what He Himself will do, is the transcript or expression of the inherent perfections of His own nature. The acts of the divine government, and the obligations of intelligent creatures, result from, and are determined by, the divine law, as their immediate or approximate cause and standard; but they all, as well as the divine law itself, are traceable to the divine nature, —to the essential perfections of God, —as their ultimate source or foundation. When, then, God issued the law denouncing death as the punishment of transgression, and thereby became pledged to inflict death on account of sin, because He had threatened, to do so, He was merely indicating or expressing a principle or purpose which was founded on, and resulted from, that inherent perfection which, in a sense, makes it necessary for Him, —although, at the same time, He acts most freely, —to give to all their due, and of course to inflict merited punishment upon sin. This is the substance of what is taught by orthodox divines when they lay down the position that punitive justice— or, as they usually call it, justitia vindicatrix— is essential to God. It is a real perfection of His nature, of which he cannot denude Himself, and which must necessarily regulate or determine the free acts of His will.

All this is in accordance with the statements of Scripture and the dictates of right reason; and these various considerations combined, fully warrant the general conclusion, that, since death has been denounced as the punishment of sin, there must be formidable obstacles in the way of sinners being pardoned and escaping from death, —that, if God should pardon sinners, some provision would be necessary for vindicating His justice and veracity, and maintaining the honour of His law;— and that the only conceivable way in which these objects could be secured, is by an adequate atonement or satisfaction rendered in the room and stead of those who had incurred the penalty of the law. Socinians have very inadequate and erroneous views of the guilt or demerit of sin, and are thus led to look upon the pardon or remission of it as a light or easy matter. But it is our duty to form our conceptions of this subject from what God has made known to us, and especially from what He has revealed to us as to the way and manner in which He must anti will treat it, ordeal with it. And all that Clod's word tells us upon this point, viewed by itself, and apart from the revelation made of an actual provision for pardoning sin and saving sinners, is fitted to impress upon us the conviction that sin fully merits, and will certainly receive, everlasting destruction from God's presence and from the glory of His power.

Another topic intimately connected with this one of the necessity of an atonement or satisfaction, —or rather, forming a part of it, —has been largely discussed in the course of this controversy, —that, namely, of the character or aspect in which God is to be regarded in dealing with sinners, with the view either of punishing them for their sins, or saving them from the punishment they have merited. Socinians, in order to show that there is no difficulty in the way of God's pardoning sin, and no necessity for an atonement or satisfaction for sin, usually represent God as acting, in this matter, either as a creditor to whom men have become debtors by sinning, or as a party who has been injured and offended by their transgressions: and then infer that, as a creditor may remit a debt if he chooses, without exacting payment, and as an injured party may forgive an injury if he chooses, without requiring any satisfaction, so, in like manner, there is no reason why God may not forgive men's sins by a mere act of His good pleasure, without any payment or compensation, either personal or vicarious. There certainly is a foundation in scriptural statements for representing sins as debts incurred to God and to His law, and also as injuries inflicted upon Him. These representations, though figurative, are, of course, intended to convey to us some ideas concerning the true state of the case; and they suggest considerations which, in some other departments of the controversy in regard to the great doctrine of the atonement, afford strong arguments against the Socinian views. But the application they make of them to disprove the necessity of an atonement, is utterly unwarranted. It is manifestly absurd to press far the resemblance or analogy between sins on the one hand, and debts or injuries on the other; or to draw inferences merely from this resemblance. These are not the only or the principal aspects in which sins are represented in Scripture.

The primary or fundamental idea of sin is, that it is a transgression of God's law, —a violation of a rule which He has commanded us to observe; and this, therefore, should be the leading aspect in which it should be contemplated, when we are considering how God will deal with it. We exclude none of the scriptural representations of sin, and none of the scriptural representations of God in His dealing with it;

but, while we take them all in, we must give prominence in our conceptions to the most important and fundamental. And as the essential idea of sin is not, that it is merely a debt or an injury, but that it is a violation of God's law, the leading character or aspect in which God ought to be contemplated when we regard Him as dealing with it, is not that of a creditor, or an injured party, who may remit the debt, or forgive the injury, as he chooses, but that of a lawgiver and a judge who has promulgated a just and righteous law, prohibiting sin under pain of death, and who is bound, by a regard to His own perfections, and the interests of holiness throughout the universe, to take care that His own character be fully vindicated, that the honour of His law be maintained, and that His moral government be firmly established; and who, therefore, cannot pardon sin, unless, in some way or other, full and adequate provision be made for securing all these objects. The pardon of sin, the forgiveness of men who have broken the law and incurred its penalty, who have done that against which God has denounced death, seems to have a strong and manifest tendency to frustrate or counteract all these objects, to stain the glory of the divine perfections, to bring dishonour upon the divine law, to shake the stability of God's moral government, and to endanger the interests of righteousness and holiness throughout the universe. And when, therefore, we contemplate God not merely as a creditor or as an injured party, but as the Supreme Lawgiver and Judge, dealing with the deliberate violation, by His intelligent and responsible creatures, of a just, and holy, and good law which he had prescribed to them, and which He had sanctioned with the threatened penalty of death, we cannot conceive it to be possible that He should pardon them without an adequate atonement or satisfaction; and we are constrained to conclude, that, if forgiveness be possible at all, it can be only on the footing of the threatened penalty being endured by another party acting in their room and stead, and of this vicarious atonement being accepted by God as satisfying His justice, and answering the claims of His law.

Whatever evidence there is for the necessity of an atonement or satisfaction, in order to the pardon of sin, of course confirms the proof of its truth or reality. It is admitted on all hands, that God does pardon sinners, —that He exempts them from punishment, receives them into His favour, and admits them to the enjoyment of eternal blessedness, notwithstanding that they have sinned and broken His law. If all that we know concerning God, His government, and law, would lead us to conclude that He could not do this without an adequate atonement or satisfaction, then we may confidently expect to find that such an atonement has been made, —that such a satisfaction has been rendered. And, on the other hand, if we have sufficient evidence of the truth and reality of an atonement as a matter of fact, —and find, moreover, that this atonement consisted of a provision so very peculiar and extraordinary as the sufferings and death, in human nature, of One who was God over all, blessed for evermore, —we are fully warranted in arguing back from such a fact to its indispensable and absolute necessity, in order to the production of the intended result; and then, from an examination of the grounds and reasons of this established necessity, we may learn much as to the true nature of this wonderful provision, and the way and manner in which it is fitted, and was designed, to accomplish its intended object.

CHAPTER THREE

THE NECESSITY AND NATURE OF THE ATONEMENT

The subject of the necessity of an atonement, in order to the pardon of sin, needs to be stated and discussed with considerable care and caution, as it is one on which there is danger of men being tempted to indulge in presumptuous speculations, and of their landing, when they follow out their speculations, in conclusions of too absolute and unqualified a kind. Some of its advocates have adopted a line of argument of which the natural result would seem to be, absolutely and universally, that sin cannot be forgiven, and, of course, that sinners cannot be saved. A mode of representation and argument about the divine justice, the principles of the divine moral government, and the divine law and veracity, which fairly leads to this conclusion, must, of course, be erroneous, since it is admitted on all hands, as a matter of fact, that sin is forgiven, that sinners are pardoned and saved. This, therefore, is an extreme to be avoided, —this is a danger to be guarded against. The considerations on which the advocates of the necessity of an atonement usually found, derived from the scriptural representations of the divine justice, law, and veracity, manifestly, and beyond all question, warrant this position, that there are very serious and formidable obstacles to the pardon of men who have broken the law, and incurred its penalty; and thus, likewise, point out what is the nature and ground of these obstacles. The difficulty lies here, that God's justice and veracity seem to impose upon Him an obligation to punish sin, and to execute His threatenings; and if this position can really be established, —and it is the foundation of the alleged necessity of an atonement or satisfaction, —the practical result would seem to be, that the law must take its course, and that the penalty must be inflicted. The argument would thus seem to prove too much, and, of course, prove nothing; a consideration well fitted to impress upon us the necessity of care and caution in stating and arguing the question, though certainly not sufficient to warrant the conclusion which some have deduced from it, —namely, that the whole argument commonly brought forward in support of the necessity of an atonement is unsatisfactory.

I have no doubt that there is truth and soundness in the argument, when rightly stated and applied. The law which God has promulgated, threatening death as the punishment of sin, manifestly throws a very serious obstacle in the way of sin being pardoned, both because it seems to indicate that God's perfections require that it be punished, and because the non-infliction of the penalty threatened seems plainly fitted to lead men to regard the law and its threatenings with indifference and contempt, —or at least to foster the conviction, that some imperfection attached to it as originally promulgated, since it had been found necessary, in the long run, to change or abrogate it, or at least to abstain from following it out, and thereby virtually to set it aside. Had God made no further revelation to men than that of the original moral law, demanding perfect obedience, with the threatened penalty of death in the event of transgression; and were the only conjecture they could form about their future destiny derived from the knowledge that they had been placed under this law, and had exposed themselves to its penalty by sinning, the conclusion which alone it would be reasonable for them to adopt, would be, that they must and would suffer the full penalty they had incurred by transgression. This is an important position, and runs directly counter to the whole substance and spirit of the Socinian views upon this subject. If, in these circumstances, —and with this position impressed upon their minds, as the only practical result of all that they then knew upon the subject, —they were further informed, upon unquestionable authority, that many sinners, —many men who had incurred the penalty of the law, —would, in point of fact, be pardoned and saved; then the conclusion which, in right reason, must be deducible from this information would be, not that the law had been abrogated or thrown aside, as imperfect or defective, but that some very peculiar and extraordinary provision had been found out and carried into effect, by which the law might be satisfied and its honour maintained, while yet those who had incurred its penalty were forgiven. And if, assuming this to be true or probable, the question were asked, What this provision could be? it would either appear to be an insoluble problem: or the only thing that could commend itself to men's reason, although reason might not itself suggest it, would be something of the nature of an atonement or satisfaction, by the substitution of another party in the room of those who had transgressed. The principles of human jurisprudence, and various incidents in the history of the world, might justify this as not unreasonable in itself, and fitted to serve some such purposes as the exigencies of the case seemed to require.

In this way, a certain train of thought, if once suggested, might be followed out, and shown to be reasonable, —to be invested, at least, with a high degree of probability; and this is just, in substance, what is commonly advocated by theologians under the head of the necessity of an atonement. There is, first, the necessity of maintaining the honour of the law, by the execution of its threatenings against transgressors; then there is the necessity of some provision for maintaining the honour of the law, if these threatenings are not, in fact, to be executed upon those who have incurred them; and then, lastly, there is the investigation of the question, —of what nature should this provision be; and what are the principles by which it must be regulated? And it is here that the investigation of the subject of the necessity of an atonement comes in, to throw some light upon its true nature and bearings.

The examination of the topics usually discussed under the head of the necessity of an atonement, viewed in connection with the undoubted truth, that many sinners are, in point of fact, pardoned and saved, leads us to expect to find some extraordinary provision made for effecting this result, and thereby gives a certain measure of antecedent probability to the allegation that such a provision has been made, and thus tends to confirm somewhat the actual evidence we may have of its truth and re- ality; while the same considerations which lead us to the conclusion that some such provision was necessary, guide us also to some inferences as to what it must consist in, and what immediate purposes it must be fitted to serve. The general substance of what is thus indicated as necessary, or as to be expected, in the nature and bearings of the provision, is this, —it must consist with, and must fully manifest all the perfections of God, and especially His justice and His hatred of sin; and it must be fitted to impress right conceptions of the perfection and unchangeableness of the divine law, and of the danger of transgressing it. God, of course, cannot do, or even permit, anything which is fitted, in its own nature, or has an inherent tendency, to convey erroneous conceptions of His character or law, of His moral government, or of the principles which regulate His dealings with His intelligent creatures; and assuredly no sinner will ever be saved, except in a way, and through a provision, in which God's justice, His hatred of sin, and His determination to maintain the honour of His law, are as fully exercised and manifested, as they would have been by the actual infliction of the full penalty which He had threatened. These perfections and qualities of God must be exercised as well as manifested, and they must be manifested as well as exercised. God must always act or regulate His volitions and procedure in accordance with the perfections and attributes of His nature, independently of any regard to His creatures, or to the impressions which they may, in point of fact, entertain with respect to Him; while it is also true that He must ever act in a way which accurately manifests His perfections, or is fitted, in its own nature, to convey to His creatures correct conceptions of what he is, and of what are the principles which regulate His dealings with them. In accordance with these principles, He must, in any provision for pardoning and saving sinners, both exercise and manifest His justice and His hatred of sin, —that is, He must act in the way which these qualities naturally and necessarily lead Him to adopt; and He must follow a course which is fitted to manifest Him to His creatures as really doing all this.

The practical result of these considerations is this, that if a provision is to be made for removing the obstacles to the pardon of sinners, —for accomplishing the objects just described, while yet sinners are saved, —there is no way in which we can conceive this to be done, except by some other suitable party taking their place, and suffering in their room and stead, the penalty they had merited. Could any such party be found, were he able and willing to do this, and were he actually to do it, then we can conceive that in this way God's justice might be satisfied, and the honour of His law maintained, because in this way the same views of the divine character, law, and government, and of the danger and demerit of sin, would be presented, as if sinners themselves had suffered the penalty in their own persons. All this, of course, implies, that the party interposing in behalf of sinners should occupy their place, and act in their room and stead, and that he should bear the penalty which they had incurred; because in this way, but in no other, so far as we can form any conception upon the subject, could the obstacles be removed, and the necessary objects be effected. And thus the general considerations on which the necessity of an atonement is maintained, are fitted to impress upon us the conviction, that there must be a true and real substitution of the party interposing to save sinners, in the room and stead of those whom he purposes to save, and the actual endurance by him of the penalty which they had incurred, and which they must, but for this interposition, have suffered.

A party qualified to interpose in behalf of sinners, in order to obtain or effect their forgiveness, by suffering in their room and stead the penalty they had deserved, must possess very peculiar qualifications indeed. The sinners to be saved were an innumerable company; the penalty which each of them had incurred was fearful and infinite, even everlasting misery; and men, of course, without revelation, are utterly incompetent to form a conception of any being who might be qualified for this. But the word of God brings before us One so peculiarly constituted and qualified, as at once to suggest the idea, that he might be able to accomplish this, —One who was God and man in one person; One who, being from eternity God, did in time assume human nature into personal union with the divine, —who assumed human nature for the purpose of saving sinners, —who was thus qualified to act as the substitute of sinners, and to endure suffering in their room; while at the same time he was qualified, by His possession of the divine nature, to give to all that he did and suffered a value and efficacy truly infinite, and fully adequate to impart to all He did a power or virtue fitted to accomplish anything, or everything, which He might intend to effect.

We formerly had occasion to show, that in regard to a subject so peculiar and extraordinary as the incarnation, sufferings, and death of the Son of God, —of One who was a possessor of the divine nature, —we are warranted in saying that, if these things really took place, they were, strictly speaking, necessary; that is, in other words, that they could not have taken place, if the object to which they were directed could possibly have been effected in any other way, or by any other means. And the mere contemplation of the fact of the sufferings and death of such a Being, independent of the full and specific information given us in Scripture as to the causes, objects, and consequences of His death, goes far to establish the truth and reality of His vicarious atoning sacrifice. When we view Him merely as a man, —but as a man, of course, perfectly free from sin, immaculately pure and holy, —we find it to be impossible to account for His sufferings upon the Socinian theory, or upon any theory but that of His suffering in the room and stead of others, and enduring the penalty which they had merited.

It is not disputed that sin is, in the case of intelligent and rational beings, the cause of suffering; and we cannot conceive that, under the government of a God of infinite power, and wisdom, and justice, and goodness, any such Being should be subjected to suffering except for sin. The suffering, —the severe and protracted suffering, —and, finally, the cruel and ignominious death of Christ, viewing Him merely as a perfectly holy and just man, are facts, the reality of which is universally admitted, and of which, therefore, all equally are called upon to give some explanation. The Socinians have no explanation to give of them. It is repugnant to all right conceptions of the principles of God's moral government, that He should inflict upon an intelligent and responsible being suffering which is not warranted or sanctioned by sin as the cause or ground of it, as that which truly justifies and explains it, —that He should inflict suffering upon a holy and innocent Being, merely in order that others may be, in some way or other, benefited by His sufferings. It is, indeed, very common, in the administration of God's moral government, that the sin of one being should be the means or occasion of bringing suffering upon others; but then it holds true, either that these others are also themselves sinners, or that they are legally liable to all the suffering that has ever been inflicted upon them, or permitted to befall them. The peculiarity in Christ's case is, that while perfectly free from sin, original as well as actual, He was yet subjected to severe suffering and to a cruel death; and this not merely by the permission, but by the special agency and appointment of God. And this was done, according to the Socinian hypothesis, merely in order that others might, in some way or other, derive benefit from the suffering and death inflicted upon Him. There is here no explanation of the admitted facts of the case, that is at all consistent with the principles of God's moral government. The doctrine of a vicarious atonement alone affords anything like an explanation of these facts; because, by means of it, we can account for them in consistency with the principle, that sin, —that is, either personal or imputed, —is the cause, the warrant, and the explanation of suffering. The Scripture assures us that Christ suffered for sin, —that He died for sin. And even viewing this statement apart from the fuller and more specific information given us in other parts of Scripture, with respect to the connection between the sin of men and the sufferings of the Saviour, and regarding it only in its relation to the general principles of God's moral government, we are warranted in concluding that sin was the impulsive and meritorious cause of His suffering; and from this we are entitled to draw the inference, that, as He had no sin of His own, he must in some way have become involved in, and responsible for, the sin of others, and that this was the cause or reason why he was subjected to death. On all these various grounds we have a great deal of general argument upon the subject of the atonement, independent of a minute and exact examination of particular scriptural statements, which tends to confirm its truth, and to illustrate its general nature and bearing.

We have seen that some of the attributes of God, and some things we know as to His moral government and law, plainly suggest to us the convictions, that there are serious obstacles to the forgiveness of sin, —that if sin is to be forgiven, some extraordinary provision must be made for the exercise and manifestation of the divine justice and holiness, so that he shall still be, and appear to be, just and holy, even while pardoning sin and admitting sinners into the enjoyment of His favour; for making His creatures see and feel, that, though they are delivered from the curse of the law which they had broken, that law is, notwithstanding, of absolute perfection, of unchangeable obligation, and entitled to all honour and respect. The only thing that has ever been conceived or suggested at all fitted to accomplish this, is, that atonement or satisfaction should be made by the endurance of the penalty of the law in the room and stead of those who should be pardoned. This seems adapted to effect the object, and thereby to remove the obstacles, while in no other way can we conceive it possible that this end can be attained.

And while the holiness, justice, and veracity of God seem to require this, there is nothing in His benevolence or placability that precludes it. The benevolence or placability of God could produce merely a readiness to forgive and to save sinners, provided this could be effected in full consistency with all the other attributes of His nature, all the principles of His moral government, and all the objects he was bound to aim at, as the Lawgiver and Governor of the universe; and these, as we have seen, throw obstacles in the way of the result being effected. The actings of God, —His actual dealings with His creatures, —must be the result of the combined exercise of all His perfections; and He cannot, in any instance, act inconsistently with any one of them. His benevolence cannot be a mere indiscriminate determination to confer happiness, and His placability cannot be a mere indiscriminate determination to forgive those who have transgressed against Him.

The Scriptures reveal to us a fact of the deepest interest, and one that ought never to be forgotten or lost sight of when we are contemplating the principles that regulate God's dealings with His creatures— namely, that some of the angels kept not their first estate, but fell by transgression; and that no provision has been made for pardoning and saving them, —no atonement or satisfaction provided for their sin, —no opportunity of escape or recovery afforded them. They sinned, or broke God's law; and their doom, in consequence, was unchangeably and eternally fixed. This is a fact, —this was the way in which God dealt with a portion of His intelligent creatures. Of course, He acted in this case in full accordance with the perfections of His nature and the principles of His government. We are bound to employ this fact, which God has revealed to us, as one of the materials which He has given us for enabling us to know Him. We are bound to believe, in regard to Him, whatever this fact implies or establishes, and to refuse to believe whatever it contradicts or precludes. And it manifestly requires us to believe this at least, that there is nothing in the essential perfections of God which affords any sufficient ground for the conclusion that he will certainly pardon transgressors of His laws, or make any provision for saving them from the just and legitimate consequences of their sins. This is abundantly manifest. And this consideration affords good ground to suspect that it was the flat contradiction which the scriptural history of the fall and fate of angels presents to the views of the Socinians, with regard to the principles of God's moral government, that has generally led them, like the Sadducees of old, to maintain that there is neither angel nor spirit, though there is evidently not the slightest appearance of unreasonableness in the general doctrine of the existence of superior spiritual beings, employed by God in accomplishing His purposes.

As, then, there is nothing in God's benevolence or placability which affords any certain ground for the conclusion that he must and will pardon sinners, so there can be nothing in these qualities inconsistent with His requiring atonement or satisfaction in order to their forgiveness, while other attributes of His nature seem plainly to demand this. God's benevolence and placability are fully manifested in a readiness to bless and to forgive, in so far as this can be done, in consistency with the other attributes of His nature, and the whole principles of His moral government. And while there is nothing in His benevolence or placability inconsistent with His requiring an atonement or satisfaction in order to forgiveness, it is further evident, that if He Himself should provide this atonement or satisfaction to His own justice and law, and be the real author and deviser of all the plans and arrangements connected with the attainment of the blessed result of forgiveness and salvation to sinners, a scheme would be presented to us which would most fully and strikingly manifest the combined glory of all the divine perfections, —in which he would show Himself to be the just God, and the justifier of the ungodly, —in which righteousness and peace should meet together, mercy and truth should embrace each other. And this is the scheme which is plainly and fully revealed to us in the word of God. Provision is made for pardoning men's sins and saving their souls, through the vicarious sufferings and death of One who was God and man in one person, and who voluntarily agreed to take their place, and to suffer in their room and stead; thus satisfying divine justice, complying with the demands of the law by enduring its penalty, and manifesting most fully the sinfulness and the danger of sin. But this was done by God Himself, who desired the salvation of sinners, and determined to effect it; and who, in consequence, sent His Son into the world to die in man's room and stead, —who spared not His own Son, but delivered Him up for us all. So that here we have a scheme for pardoning and saving sinners which, from its very nature, must be effectual, and which not only is in full accordance with the perfections of God, but most gloriously illustrates them all. The apostle says expressly, "that God set forth His Son to be a propitiation through faith in His blood, to declare His righteousness," or with a view to the demonstration of His righteousness; and it is true that the shedding of Christ's blood as a propitiation, viewed with reference to its necessity and proper nature, does declare God's righteousness, or justice and holiness; while, viewed in its originating motives and glorious results, it most fully declares God's marvellous love to the children of men, and His determination to save sinners with an everlasting salvation.

Chapter Four

OBJECTIONS TO THE DOCTRINE OF ATONEMENT

The proper order to be followed in the investigation of this subject, or indeed of any great scriptural doctrine, is the same as that which I stated and explained in considering the doctrine of the Trinity, —namely, that we should first ascertain, by a full and minute examination of all the scriptural statements bearing upon the subject, what the Bible teaches regarding it; and then consider the general objections that may be adduced against it, taking care to keep them in their proper place, as objections, and to be satisfied with showing that they cannot be proved to have any weight; and if they should appear to be really relevant and well-founded, and not mere sophisms or difficulties, applying them, as sound reason dictates, not in the way of reversing the judgment already formed upon the appropriate evidence as to what it is that the Bible really teaches, but in the way of rejecting a professed revelation that teaches doctrines which can, ex hypothexi, be conclusively disproved.

But as the objections made by Socinians to the doctrine of the atonement are chiefly connected with some of those general and abstract topics to which we have already had occasion to advert, it may be most useful and convenient to notice them now, especially as the consideration of them is fitted, like that of the necessity of an atonement, already considered, to throw some light upon the general nature and import of the doctrine itself.

Many of the objections commonly adduced against the doctrine of atonement are mere cavils, —mere exhibitions of unwarranted presumption, —and are sufficiently disposed of by the general considerations of the exalted and incomprehensible nature of the subject itself, and of the great mystery of godliness, God made manifest in the flesh, on which it is based. These it is unnecessary to dwell upon, after the exposition of the general principles applicable to the investigation of these subjects which we have already given. Some are founded upon misrepresentations of the real bearing, objects, and effects of the atonement, especially in its relation to the character and moral government of God. Nothing, for instance, is more common than for Socinians to represent the generally received doctrine of atonement as implying that God the Father is an inexorable tyrant, who insisted upon the rigorous execution of the threatenings of the law until Christ interposed, and by His offering up of Himself satisfied God's demands, and thereby introduced into the divine mind a totally different state of feeling in regard to sinners, —the result of which was, that He pardoned in place of punishing them. This, of course, is not the doctrine of the atonement, but a mere caricature of it. Scripture plainly teaches, —and the advocates of an atonement maintain, not only as being perfectly consistent with their doctrine, but as a constituent part of it, —that love to men, and a desire to save them from ruin, existed eternally in the divine mind, —resulting from the inherent perfections of God's nature, —that this love and compassion led Him to devise and execute a plan of salvation, and to send His Son to save sinners by offering an atonement for their sins. The atonement, then, was the consequence, and not the cause, of God's love to men, and of His desire to save them. It introduced no feeling into the divine mind which did not exist there before; though it certainly removed obstacles which other principles of His nature and government interposed to the full outflowing of the love and compassion which existed, and opened up a channel by which God, in full accordance with, and in glorious illustration of, all His perfections, might bestow upon men pardon and all other spiritual blessings, and finally eternal life. This is all that can be meant by the scriptural statements about the turning away of God's anger and His reconciliation to men, when these are ascribed to the interposition and atonement of Christ. This is all that the defenders of an atonement understand by these statements. There is nothing in their views upon this, or upon any other subject, that requires them to understand these statements in any other sense; and thus understood, they are fully accordant both with the generally received doctrine of the atonement, and with everything else that Scripture teaches concerning God, and concerning the principles that regulate His dealings with men. This objection, then, though it has been repeated constantly from the time of Socinus till the present day, is founded wholly upon a misrepresentation of the doctrine objected to, —a misrepresentation for which there is no warrant or excuse whatever, except, perhaps, the declamations of some ignorant and injudicious preachers of the doctrine, who have striven to represent it in the way they thought best fitted to impress the popular mind.

The only objections of a general kind to the doctrine of an atonement that are entitled to any notice are these: First, that it involves injustice, by representing the innocent as punished in the room of the guilty, and the guilty thereby escaping; secondly, that it is inconsistent with the free grace, or gratuitous favour, which the Scriptures ascribe to God in the remission of men's sins; and, thirdly, that it is fitted to injure the interests of holiness, or morality. We shall very briefly advert to these in succession, but without attempting anything like a full discussion of them.

First, It is alleged to be unjust to punish the innocent in the room of the guilty, and on this ground to allow the transgressors to escape. Now, the defenders of the doctrine of atonement admit that it does assume or imply the state of matters which is here described, and represented as unjust, —namely, the punishment of the innocent in the room of the guilty. Some of them, indeed, scruple about the application of the terms punishment and penal to the sufferings and death of Christ. But this scrupulosity appears to me to be frivolous and vexatious, resting upon no sufficient ground, and serving no good purpose. If men, indeed, begin with defining punishment to mean the infliction of suffering upon an offender on account of his offence, —thus including the actual personal demerit of the sufferer in the idea which the word conveys, —they settle the question of the penalty, or penal character, of Christ's suffering by the mere definition. In this sense, of course, Christ's sufferings were not penal. But the definition is purely arbitrary, and is not required by general usage, which warrants us in regarding and describing as penal any suffering inflicted judicially, or in the execution of the provisions of law, on account of sin. And this arbitrary restriction of the meaning of the terms punishment and penal is of no use, although some of those who have recourse to it seem to think so, in warding off Socinian objections;— because, in the first place, there is really nothing in the doctrine of the atonement worth contending for, if it be not true that Christ endured, in the room and stead of sinners, the suffering which the law demanded of them on account of their sins, and which, but for His enduring it, as their substitute, they must themselves have endured, —and because, in the second place, the allegation of injustice applies, with all the force it has, to the position just stated, whether Christ's sufferings be called penal or not.

With regard to the objection itself, the following are the chief considerations to be attended to, by the exposition and application of which it is fully disposed of: First, that, as we have already had occasion to state and explain in a different connection, the sufferings and death of an innocent person in this matter are realities which all admit, and which all equally are bound to explain. Christ's sufferings were as great upon the Socinian, as upon the orthodox, theory with regard to their cause and object; while our doctrine of His being subjected to suffering because of the sin of others being imputed to Him, or laid upon Him, brings the facts of the case into accordance with some generally recognised principles of God's moral government, which, upon the Socinian scheme, is impossible. The injustice, of course, is not alleged to be in the fact that Christ, an innocent person, was subjected to so much suffering, —for there remains the same fact upon any hypothesis, —but in His suffering in the room and stead of sinners, with the view, and to the effect, of their escaping punishment.

Now, we observe, secondly, that this additional circumstance of His suffering being vicarious and expiatory, —which may be said to constitute our theory as to the grounds, causes, or objects of His suffering, —in place of introducing an additional difficulty into the matter, is the only thing which contributes in any measure to explain it. And it does contribute in some measure to explain it, because it can be shown to accord with the ordinary principles of enlightened reason to maintain, —first, that it is not of the essence of the idea of punishment, that it must necessarily, and in every instance, be inflicted upon the very person who has committed the sin that calls for it; or, as it is expressed by Grotius, who has applied the recognised principles of jurisprudence and law to this subject with great ability: "Notandum est, esse quidem essentiale poenoe, ut infligatur ob peccatum, sed non item essentiale ei esse ut infligatur ipsi qui peccavit — and, secondly, that substitution and satisfaction, in the matter of inflicting punishment, are to some extent recognised in the principles of human jurisprudence, and in the arrangements of human governments; while there is much also, in the analogies of God's providential government of the world, to sanction them, or to afford answers to the allegations of their injustice.

Thirdly, the transference of penal suffering, or suffering judicially inflicted in accordance with the provisions of law, from one party to another, cannot be proved to be universally and in all cases unjust. No doubt, an act of so peculiar a kind, —involving, as it certainly does, a plain deviation from the ordinary regular course of procedure, —requires, in each case, a distinct and specific ground or cause to warrant it. But there are, at least, two cases in which this transference of penal suffering on account of sin from one party to another is generally recognised as just, and in which, at least, it can be easily proved, that all ground is removed for charging it with injustice. These are, —first, when the party who is appointed to suffer on account of the sin of another, has himself become legally liable to a charge of guilt, adequate to account for all the suffering inflicted; and, secondly, when he voluntarily consents to occupy the place of the offender, and to bear, in his room, the punishment which he had merited. In these cases, there is manifestly no injustice in the transference of penal suffering, so far as the parties more immediately affected are concerned; and if the general and public ends of punishment are at the same time fully provided for by the transference, or notwithstanding the transference, then there is, in these cases, no injustice of any kind committed.

The second of these cases is that which applies to the sufferings and death of Christ. He willingly agreed to stand in the room and stead of sinners, and to bear the punishment which they had merited. And if there be no injustice generally in Christ— though perfectly innocent— suffering so much as He endured, and no injustice in this suffering being penally inflicted upon Him on account of the sins of others, —His own free consent to occupy their place and to bear the punishment due to their sins being interposed, —there can be no injustice in the only other additional idea involved in our doctrine, —namely, that this suffering, inflicted upon Him, is appointed and proclaimed as the ground or means of exempting the offenders from the punishment they had deserved; or, as it is put by Grotius, "Cum per hos modos" (the cases previously mentioned, the consent of the substitute being one of them), "actus factus est licitus, quo minus deinde ordinetur ad poenam peccati alieni, nihil intercedit, modo inter eum qui peccavit et puniendum aliqua sit conjunctio." The only parties who would be injured or treated unjustly by this last feature in the case, are the lawgiver and the community (to apply the principle to the case of human jurisprudence); and if the honour and authority of the law, and the general interests of the community, are fully provided for by means of, or notwithstanding, the transference of the penal infliction, —as we undertake to prove is the case with respect to the vicarious and expiatory suffering of Christ, —then the whole ground for the charge of injustice is taken away.

The second objection is, that the doctrine of atonement or satisfaction is inconsistent with the scriptural representations of the gratuitousness of forgiveness, —of the freeness of the grace of God in pardoning sinners. It is said that God exercises no grace or free favour in pardoning sin, if He has received full satisfaction for the offences of those whom He pardons. This objection is not confined to Socinians. They adduce it against the doctrine of atonement or satisfaction altogether; while Arminians, and others who hold the doctrine of universal or indefinite atonement, adduce it against those higher, stricter, and more accurate views of substitution and satisfaction with which the doctrine of a definite or limited atonement stands necessarily connected. When they are called to deal with this Socinian objection, they usually admit that the objection is unanswerable, as adduced against the stricter views of substitution and satisfaction held by most Calvinists; while they contend that it is of no force in opposition to their modified and more rational views upon this subject, —an admission by which, as it seems to me, they virtually, in effect though not in intention, betray the whole cause of the atonement into the hands of the Socinians. As this objection has been stated and answered in our Confession of Faith, we shall follow its guidance in making a few observations upon it.

It is there said, "Christ, by His obedience and death, did fully discharge the debt of all those that are thus justified, and did make a proper, real, and full satisfaction to His Father's justice in their behalf." Here the doctrine of substitution and satisfaction is fully and explicitly declared in its highest and strictest sense. But the authors of the Confession were not afraid of being able to defend, in perfect consistency with this, the free grace, the gratuitous mercy of God, in justifying, —that is, in pardoning and accepting sinners. And, accordingly, they go on to say, "Yet, inasmuch as he was given by the Father for them, and His obedience and satisfaction accepted in their stead, and both freely, not for anything in them, their justification is only of free grace; that both the exact justice and rich grace of God might be glorified in the justification of sinners." Now, the grounds here laid for maintaining the free grace of God in the forgiveness of sinners, notwithstanding that a full atonement or satisfaction was made for their transgressions, are two: first, that Christ, the atoner or satisfier, was given by the Father for them, —that is, that the Father Himself devised and provided the atonement or satisfaction, —provided it, so to speak, at His own cost.— by not sparing His own Son, but delivering Him up for us all. If this be true, —if men had no right whatever to such a provision, —if they had done, and could do, nothing whatever to merit or procure it, —then this consideration must necessarily render the whole of the subsequent process based upon it, in its bearing upon men, purely gratuitous, —altogether of free grace, —unless, indeed, at some subsequent stage, men should be able to do something meritorious and efficacious for themselves in the matter. But then, secondly, God not only freely provided the satisfaction, —He likewise, when it was rendered by Christ, accepted it in the room of all those who are pardoned, and this, too, freely, or without anything in them, —that is, without their having done, or being able to do, anything to merit or procure it, or anything which it involves. Pardon, therefore, and acceptance are freely or gratuitously given to men, though they were purchased by Christ, who paid the price of His precious blood. The scriptural statements about the free grace of God in pardoning and accepting men, on which the objection is founded, assert or imply only the gratuitousness of the blessings in so far as the individuals who ultimately receive them are concerned, and contain nothing whatever that, either directly or by implication, denies that they were purchased by Christ, by the full satisfaction which he rendered in the room and stead of those who finally partake of them; while the gratuitousness of God's grace in the matter, viewed as an attribute or quality of His, is fully secured and manifested by His providing and accepting the satisfaction.

These considerations are amply sufficient to answer the Socinian objection about free grace and gratuitous remission, even on the concession of the strictest views of the substitution and satisfaction of Christ; and without dwelling longer on this subject, I would merely remark in general, that it holds true equally of the grounds of this Socinian objection, and of the concession made to it by Arminians and other defenders of universal atonement, —the concession, namely, that it is unanswerable upon the footing of the stricter views of substitution and satisfaction; and indeed, I may say, it holds true generally of the grounds of the opposition made to the doctrine of definite or limited atonement, —that they are chiefly based upon the unwarrantable practice of taking up the different parts or branches of the scheme of redemption, as unfolded in Scripture, separately, and viewing them in isolation from each other, in place of considering them together, as parts of one great whole, and in their relation to each other and to the entire scheme.

The third and last objection to which we proposed to advert is, that the doctrine of the atonement is fitted to injure the interests of holiness or morality. The general ground on which this allegation is commonly made is, —that the introduction of an atonement or satisfaction by another party is held to release men from the obligations of the moral law; and that the general tendency of the doctrine is to lead men to be careless and indifferent about the regulation of their conduct and their growth in holiness. This is just the common objection usually made to the whole scheme of the doctrines of grace; and in this, as well as in other applications of it, it can be easily shown that the objection proceeds upon an erroneous and defective view of the state of the case, and upon a low and grovelling sense of the motives by which men are, or should be, animated. The whole extent to which the atonement or satisfaction of Christ affects men's relation to the law is this, that men are exempted from paying, in their own persons, the penalty they had incurred, and are saved from its infliction by its being borne by another in their room and stead. Now, there is certainly nothing in this which has any appearance of relaxing the obligation of the law as a rule or standard which they are bound to follow. There is nothing in this which has any tendency to convey the impression that God is unconcerned about the honour of His law, or that we may trifle with its requirements with impunity. The whole object and tendency of the doctrine of atonement is to convey the very opposite views and impressions with regard to the law, —the obligation which it imposes, and the respect and reverence which are due to it.

In order to form a right conception of the moral tendency of a doctrine, we must conceive of the case of a man who understands and believes it, —who is practically applying it according to its true nature and tendency, and living under its influence, —and then consider how it is fitted to operate upon his character, motives, and actions. And to suppose that the doctrine of the atonement, understood, believed, and applied, can lead men to be careless about regulating their conduct according to God's law, is to regard them as incapable of being influenced by any other motive than a concern about their own safety— to imagine that, having attained to a position of safety, they must thenceforth be utterly uninfluenced by anything they have ever learned or heard about God, and sin, and His law, and eternity, and totally unmoved by any benefits that have been conferred upon them. When men adduce this objection against the doctrine of the atonement, they unconsciously make a manifestation of their own character and motives. In bringing forward the objection, they are virtually saying, "If we believed the doctrine of the atonement, we would certainly lead very careless and immoral lives." And here I have no doubt they are speaking the truth, according to their present views and motives. But this of course implies a virtual confession, —first, that any outward decency which their conduct may at present exhibit, is to be traced solely to the fear of punishment; and, secondly, that if they were only secured against punishment, they would find much greater pleasure in sin than in holiness, much greater satisfaction in serving the devil than in serving God; and that they would never think of showing any gratitude to Him who had conferred the safety and deliverance on which they place so much reliance. Socinians virtually confess all this, with respect to their own present character and motives, when they charge the doctrine of the atonement with a tendency unfavourable to the interests of morality. But if men's character and motives are, as they should be, influenced by the views they have been led to form concerning God and His law; if they are capable of being affected by the contemplation of noble and exalted objects, by admiration of excellence, and by a sense of thankfulness for benefits, —instead of being animated solely by a mere desire to secure their own safety and comfort, —they must find in the doctrine of the atonement, —and in the conceptions upon all important subjects which it is fitted to form, —motives amply sufficient to lead them to hate sin, to fear and love God, to cherish affection and gratitude towards Him who came in God's name to seek and to save them, and to set their affections on things above, where He sitteth at the right hand of God. These are the elements from which alone— as is proved both by the nature of the case and the experience of the world— anything like high and pure morality will ever proceed; and no position of this nature can be more certain, than that the believers in the doctrine of the atonement have done much more in every way to adorn the doctrine of our God and Saviour, than those who have denied it.

There is, then, no real weight in the objections commonly adduced against the doctrine of the atonement. Not that there are not difficulties connected with the subject, which we are unable fully to solve; but there is nothing so formidable as to tempt us to make a very violent effort— and that, certainly, is necessary— in the way of distorting and perverting Scripture, in order to get rid of it; and nothing to warrant us in rejecting the divine authority of the Bible, because it establishes this doctrine with such full and abundant evidence. We have already seen a good deal, in considerations derived from what we know concerning the divine character and moral government, fitted to lead us to believe, by affording at least the strongest probabilities and presumptions, that the method of an atonement or satisfaction might be that which would be adopted for pardoning and saving sinners; and that this method really involves the substitution of the Son of God in the room and stead of those who are saved by Him, and His endurance, as their surety and substitute, of the punishment which they had deserved by their sin. But the full proof of this great doctrine is to be found only in a minute and careful examination of the meaning of scriptural statements; and in the prosecution of this subject, it has been conclusively proved that the generally received doctrine of the atonement is so thoroughly established by Scripture, and so interwoven with its whole texture, that they must stand or fall together; and that any man who denies the substance of the common doctrine upon this subject, would really act a much more honest and rational part than Socinians generally do, if he would openly deny that the Bible is to be regarded as the rule of faith, or as entitled to reverence or respect as a communication from God.

CHAPTER FIVE

SCRIPTURAL EVIDENCE FOR THE ATONEMENT

We cannot enter into anything like an exposition of the Scripture evidence in support of the commonly received doctrine of the atonement, the general nature and import of which we have endeavoured to explain. This evidence is collected from the whole field of Scripture, and comprehends a great extent and variety of materials, every branch of which has, upon both sides, been subjected to a thorough critical investigation. The evidence bearing upon this great doctrine may be said to comprehend all that is contained in Scripture upon the subject of sacrifices, from the commencement of the history of our fallen race; all that is said about the nature, causes, and consequences of the sufferings and death of Christ; and all that is revealed as to the way and manner in which men do, in point of fact, obtain or receive the forgiveness of their sins, or exemption from the penal consequences to which their sins have exposed them. The general observations which we have already made about the Socinian mode of dealing with and interpreting Scripture, and the illustrations we gave of these general observations in their application to the doctrine of the Trinity and the person of Christ, —the substance of all that we have stated in the way of explaining both how scriptural statements should and should not be dealt with, and what are the principles which, in right reason, though in opposition to self-styled rationalism, ought to regulate this matter, —are equally applicable to the subject of the atonement— are equally illustrative of the way in which the scriptural statements bearing upon this point should, and should not, be treated and applied. I shall therefore say nothing more on these general topics. The few observations which I have to make on the scriptural evidence in support of the doctrine of the atonement, must be restricted to the object of giving some hints or suggestions as to the way in which this subject ought to be investigated, pointing out some of the leading divisions under which the evidences may be classed, and the leading points that must be attended to and kept in view in examining it.

That Christ suffered and died for our good, and in order to benefit us, —in order that thereby sinners might be pardoned and saved, —and that by suffering and dying He has done something or other intended and fitted to contribute to the accomplishment of this object, —is, of course, admitted by all who profess to believe, in any sense, in the divine origin of the Christian revelation. And the main question discussed in the investigation of the subject of the atonement really resolves, as I formerly explained, into this: What is the relation actually subsisting between the death of Christ and the forgiveness of men's sins I In what way does the one bear upon and affect the other? Now, the doctrine which has been generally received in the Christian church upon this all-important question is this: That Christ, in order to save men from sin and its consequences, voluntarily took their place, and suffered and died in their room and stead; that He offered up Himself a sacrifice for them; that His death was a punishment inflicted upon Him because they had deserved death; that it was in a fair and reasonable sense the penalty which they had incurred; that by suffering death as a penal infliction in their room and stead, He has satisfied the claims or demands of the divine justice and the divine law; and by making satisfaction in their room, has expiated or atoned for their sins, and has thus procured for them redemption and reconciliation with God.

The scriptural proof of this position overturns at once both the Socinian theory, —which restricts the efficacy of Christ's sufferings and death to their fitness for confirming and establishing truths, and supplying motives and encouragements to repentance and holiness, which are with them the true grounds or causes of the forgiveness of sinners, —and also the theory commonly held by the Arians, which, without including the ideas of substitution and satisfaction, represents Christ as, in some way or other, acquiring by His suffering and death a certain influence with God, which he employs in obtaining for men the forgiveness of their sins. The proof of the generally received doctrine overturns at once both these theories, not by establishing directly and positively that they are false, —for, as I formerly explained in the general statement of this subject, they are true so far as they go, —but by showing that they do not contain the whole truth; that they embody only the smallest and least important part of what Scripture teaches; and that there are other ideas fully warranted by Scripture, and absolutely necessary in order to anything like a complete and correct representation of the whole Scripture doctrine upon the subject.

One of the first and most obvious considerations that occurs in directing our attention to the testimony of Scripture upon the subject is, that neither the Socinian nor the Arian doctrine is reconcilable with the peculiarity and the immediateness of the connection which the general strain of scriptural language indicates as subsisting between the death of Christ and the forgiveness of sinners; while all this is in fullest harmony with the orthodox doctrine. If the death of Christ bears upon the forgiveness of sin only indirectly and remotely through the medium or intervention of the way in which it bears upon men's convictions, motives, and conduct, and if it bears upon this result only in a way in which other causes or influences, and even other things contained in the history of Christ Himself, do or might equally bear upon it, —and all this is implied in the denial of the doctrine of the atonement, —then it seems impossible to explain why in Scripture such special and peculiar importance is ascribed to Christ's death in this matter; why the forgiveness of sin is never ascribed to any other cause or source of right views or good motives, —such, for instance, as Christ's teaching, or His resurrection; and why the death of Christ and the remission of men's sins are so constantly represented as most closely and immediately connected with each other. This constitutes a very strong presumption in favour of the generally received doctrine upon the subject; but in order to establish it thoroughly, it is necessary to examine carefully and minutely the meaning of the specific statements of Scripture which make known to us the nature, objects, and consequences of Christ's death, and the actual connection between it and the forgiveness of sin. And we would now briefly indicate the chief heads under which they may be classed, and some of the principal points to be attended to in the investigation of them.

First, we would notice that there are some important words, on the true and proper meaning of which the settlement of this controversy essentially depends, and of which, therefore, the meaning must be carefully investigated, and, if possible, fully ascertained. The words to which I refer are such as these: atonement, —used frequently in the Old Testament in connection with the sacrifices, and once (i.e., in our version) in the New Testament; bearing and carrying, as applied to sin; propitiation, reconciliation, redemption, etc. The words which express these ideas in the original Hebrew or Greek, —such as, hattath, asham, kopher, nasa, sabal, in Hebrew; and in Greek, ἱλάω or ἱλάσκομαι, and its derivatives, ἱλάσμος and ἱλάστήριον, καταλλάσσω and καταλλαγή, ἀγοράζω, λυτρόω, λυτρον, ἀντίλυτρον, φέρω, and ἀναφέρω, —have all been subjected to a thorough critical investigation in the course of this controversy; and no one can be regarded as well versant in its merits, and able to defend the views which he has been led to adopt, unless he has examined the meaning of these words, and can give some account of the philological grounds on which his conclusions, as to their import, are founded. Under this head may be also comprehended the different Greek prepositions which are commonly translated in our version by the word for, in those statements in which Christ is represented as dying for sins, and dying for sinners, —viz., διὰ, περί, υττέρ, and ἀντί, —for much manifestly depends upon their true import.

The object to be aimed at in the investigation of these words is, of course, to ascertain, by a diligent and careful application of the right rules and materials, what is their natural, obvious, ordinary import, as used by the sacred writers, —what sense they were fitted, and must therefore have been intended, to convey to those to whom they were originally addressed. It can scarcely be disputed that these words, in their obvious and ordinary meaning, being applied to the death of Christ, decidedly support the generally received doctrine of the atonement; and the substance of what Socinians, and other opponents of the doctrine, usually labour to establish in regard to them is, that there are some grounds for maintaining that they may bear, because they sometimes mast bear, a different sense, —a sense in which they could not sanction the doctrine of the atonement; so that the points to be attended to in this department of the discussion are these: First, to scrutinize the evidence adduced, that the particular word under consideration must sometimes be taken in a different sense from that which it ordinarily bears; secondly, to see whether, in the passages in which, if taken in its ordinary sense, it would sanction the doctrine of the atonement, there be any necessity, or even warrant, for departing from this ordinary meaning. The proof of a negative upon either of these two points is quite sufficient to overturn the Socinian argument, and to leave the passages standing in full force as proofs of the orthodox doctrine; while, in regard to many of the most important passages, the defenders of that doctrine have not only proved a negative upon these two questions, —that is, upon one or other of them, —but have further established, thirdly, that, upon strictly critical grounds, the ordinary meaning of the word is that which ought to be there adopted.

But we must proceed to consider and classify statements, as distinguished from mere words, though these words enter into most of the important statements upon the subject; and here I would be disposed to place first those passages in which Christ is represented as executing the office of a Priest, and as offering up Himself as a sacrifice. That he is so represented cannot be disputed. The question is, What ideas with respect to the nature, objects, and effects of His death, was this representation intended to convey to us? The New Testament statements concerning the priesthood and sacrifice of Christ are manifestly connected with, are in some sense taken from, and must be in some measure interpreted by, the accounts given of the priesthood and sacrifices under the law, and of the origin and objects of sacrifices generally, —in so far as they can be regarded as affording any indication of the principles which regulate the divine procedure with respect to the forgiveness of sin. This opens up a wide and interesting field of discussion, —historical and critical, —comprehending not only all that we learn from Scripture upon the subject, but likewise anything to be gathered from the universal prevalence of sacrifices among heathen nations, and the notions which mankind have generally associated with them.

The substance of what is usually contended for upon this topic by Socinians and other opponents of the doctrine of the atonement is this, —that animal sacrifices were not originally appointed and required by God, but were devised and invented by men, —that they were natural and appropriate expressions of men's sense of their dependence upon God, their unworthiness of His mercies, their penitence for their sins, and their obligations to Him for His goodness; but that they were not generally understood to involve or imply any idea of substitution or satisfaction, —of propitiating God, and of expiating or atoning for sin: that they were introduced by God into the Mosaic economy, because of their general prevalence, and their capacity of being applied to some useful purposes of instruction; but that no additional ideas were then connected with them beyond what had obtained in substance in heathen nations: that the Levitical sacrifices were not regarded as vicarious and propitiating; and that their influence or effect, such as it was, was confined to ceremonial, and did not extend to moral offences: that the statements in the New Testament in which Christ is represented as officiating as a Priest, and as offering a sacrifice, are mere allusions of a figurative or metaphorical kind to the Levitical sacrifices, employed in accommodation to Jewish notions and habits; and that, more especially, the minute and specific statements upon this subject, contained in the Epistle to the Hebrews, are, as the Improved or Socinian version, published about forty years ago, says, characterized by "far-fetched analogies and inaccurate reasonings." In opposition to all this, the defenders of the doctrine of the atonement generally contend that animal sacrifices were of divine appointment, and were intended by God to symbolize, to represent, and to teach the great principles which regulate His conduct in regard to sin and sinners, —that they expressed a confession of sin on the part of the person by, or for, whom they were offered, —that they indicated the transference of his sin, and the punishment it merited, to the victim offered, the endurance of the punishment by the victim in the room of the offerer, —and, as the result, the exemption of the offerer from the punishment he deserved; in other words, that they were vicarious, as implying the substitution of one for the other, and expiatory or propitiatory, as implying the oblation and the acceptance of a satisfaction, or compensation, or equivalent for the offence, and, as a consequence, its remission, —that these ideas, though intermingled with much error, are plainly enough exhibited in the notions which prevailed on the subject among heathen nations, and are fully sanctioned by the statements made with respect to the nature, objects, and consequences of the divinely appointed sacrifices of the Mosaic economy;— that these were evidently vicarious and expiatory, —that they were appointed to be offered chiefly for ceremonial, but also for some moral offences, considered as violations of the ceremonial law, though, of course, they could not of themselves really expiate or atone for the moral, but only the ceremonial, guilt of this latter class, —that they really expiated or removed ceremonial offences, or were accepted as a ground or reason for exempting men from the punishment incurred by the violation or neglect of the provisions of the Jewish theocracy, while their bearing upon moral offences could be only symbolical or typical;— that, in place of the New Testament statements about the priesthood and sacrifice of

Christ being merely figurative allusions to the Levitical sacrifices, the whole institution of sacrifices, and the place which they occupied in the Mosaic economy, were regulated and determined by a regard to the one sacrifice of Christ, —that they were intended to direct men's faith to it, —that they embodied and represented the principles on which its efficacy depended, and should therefore be employed in illustrating its true nature and bearings; while everything to be learned from them, in regard to it, is fitted to impress upon us the conviction, that it was vicarious and expiatory, —that is, presented and accepted in the room and stead of others, and thus effecting or procuring their reconciliation to God, and their exemption from the penal consequences of their sins. All this has been maintained, and all this has been established, by the defenders of the doctrine of the atonement; and with the principal grounds on which these various positions rest, and on which they can be defended from the objections of adversaries, and from the opposite views taken by them upon these points, all students of Scripture ought to possess some acquaintance. The most important and fundamental of the various topics comprehended in this wide field of discussion, are involved in the settlement of these two questions, —namely, first, What was the character, object, and immediate effect of the Levitical sacrifices? were they vicarious and expiatory, or not? and, secondly, What is the true relation between the scriptural statements concerning the Levitical sacrifices, and those concerning the sacrifice of Christ? and what light does anything we know concerning the former throw upon the statements concerning the latter? These are questions presenting materials for much interesting discussion; and it is our duty to seek to possess some knowledge of the facts and arguments by which they are to be decided.

Secondly, another important class of passages consists of those which bear directly and immediately upon the true nature and the immediate object of Christ's death. There are some general considerations derived from Scripture, to which we have already had occasion to refer, which afford good ground for certain inferences upon this subject. If it was the death, in human nature, of One who was also a possessor of the divine nature, as Scripture plainly teaches, then it must possess a nature, character, and tendency altogether peculiar and extraordinary; and must be fitted, and have been intended, to effect results altogether beyond the range of what could have been accomplished by anything that is competent to any creature, —results directly related to infinity and eternity. If it was the death of One who had no sin of His own, who was perfectly innocent and holy, we are constrained to conclude that it must have been inflicted upon account of the sins of others, whose punishment he agreed to bear. A similar conclusion has been deduced from some of the actual features of Christ's sufferings as described in Scripture, especially from His agony in the garden, and His desertion upon the cross; circumstances which it is not easy to explain, if His sufferings were merely those of a martyr and an exemplar, —and which naturally suggest the propriety of ascribing to them a very different character and object, and are obviously fitted to lead us to conceive of Him as enduring the punishment of sin, inflicted by God, in the execution of the provisions of His holy law.

But the class of passages to which we now refer, are those which contain distinct and specific information as to the real nature, character, and immediate object of His sufferings and death; such as those which assure us that He suffered and died for sin and for sinners; that He bore our sins, and took them away; that He was wounded for our transgressions, and bruised for our iniquities; that He suffered for sin, the just for the unjust; that He was made sin for us; that He was made a curse for us, etc. Such statements as these abound in Scripture; and the question is, What ideas

are they fitted— and therefore, as we must believe, intended— to convey
to us concerning the true nature and character of Christ's death, and its
relation to, and bearing upon, our sin, and the forgiveness of it? Now, if
we attend to these statements, and, instead of being satisfied with vague
and indefinite conceptions of their import, seek to realize their meaning,
and to understand distinctly what is their true sense and signification,
we must be constrained to conclude that, if they have any meaning, they
were intended to impress upon us the convictions— that our sin was
the procuring cause of Christ's death, that which rendered His death
necessary, and actually brought it about, —that He consented to occupy
the place of sinners, and to bear the punishment which they had deserved
and incurred, —that, in consequence, their guilt, in the sense of legal
answerableness or liability to punishment (reatus), was transferred to,
and laid on, Him; so that He suffered, in their room and stead, the
punishment which they had deserved and incurred, and which, but for
His enduring it, they must have suffered in their own persons. And as
this is the natural and obvious meaning of the scriptural statements,
—that which, as a matter of course, they would convey to any one who
would attend to them, and seek to realize clearly and definitely the ideas
which they are fitted to express, —so it is just the meaning which, after
all the learning, ingenuity, and skill of adversaries have been exerted in
obscuring and perverting them, comes out more palpably and certainly
than before, as the result of the most searching critical investigation.

Suffering and dying for us means, according to the Socinians. merely
suffering and dying on our account, for our good, with a view to our
being benefited by it. It is true that Christ died for us in this sense; but
this is not the whole of what the scriptural statements upon the subject
are fitted to convey. It can be shown that they naturally and properly
express the idea that He died in our room and stead, and thus constrain

us to admit the conception of His substitution for us, or of His being put in our place, and being made answerable for us. The prepositions translated for, —when persons, tee or sinners, are the objects of the relation indicated, — are διά, ὑπέρ, and ἀντί. Now, it is admitted that διά naturally and properly means, on our account, or for our benefit, and does not of itself suggest anything else. It is admitted, further, that ὑπέρ may mean, on our account, as well as in our room, though the latter is its more ordinary signification, —that which it most readily suggests, —and that which, in many cases, the connection shows to be the only one that is admissible. But it is contended that ἀντί, which is also employed for this purpose, means, and can mean only, in this connection, instead of, or in the room of, as denoting the substitution of one party in place of another. This does not warrant us in holding that, wherever διά and ὑπέρ are employed, they, too, must imply substitution of one for another, since it is also true that Christ died for our benefit, or on our account; but it does warrant us to assert that the ordinary meaning of διά, and the meaning which may sometimes be assigned to ὑπέρ, —namely, on account of, —does not bring out the whole of what the Scripture teaches with respect to the relation subsisting between the death of Christ and those for whose benefit it was intended.

The prepositions employed when sins, and not persons, are represented as the causes or objects of Christ's suffering or dying, are διά, ὑπέρ, and περί; and it is contended and proved, that, according to Scripture, what the proper ordinary meaning of dying for or on account of sin, — διά, ὑπέρ, περί, ἁμαρτίαν, or ἁμαρτίας, —is this, —that the sin spoken of was that which procured and merited the death, so that the death was a penal infliction on account of the sin which caused it, or for which it was endured. Bearing or carrying sin, it can be proved, has, for its ordinary meaning in Scripture, being made, or becoming legally answerable for sin, and, in consequence, enduring its punishment. There are, indeed, some other words used in Scripture in regard to this matter, which are somewhat more indeterminate in their meaning, and cannot be proved of themselves to import more than the Socinian sense of bearing sin, —namely, taking it away, or generally removing it and its consequences, such as nasa in the Old Testament, and αἴρω in the New; but sabal in the Old Testament, and φέρω or ἀναφέρω in the New, have no such indefiniteness of meaning. They include, indeed, the idea of taking away or removing, which the Socinians regard as the whole of their import; but it can be proved that their proper meaning is to bear or carry, and thus by bearing or carrying, to remove or take away. As to the statements, that Christ was wounded for our transgressions, and bruised for our iniquities, that he was made sin and made a curse for us, and others of similar import, there is really nothing adduced, possessed even of plausibility, against their having the meaning which they naturally and properly convey, —namely, that our liability to punishment for sin was transferred to Him, and that He, in consequence, endured in our room and stead what we had deserved and incurred.

Thirdly, The third and last class of passages consists of those which describe the effects or results of Christ's death, —the consequences which have flowed from it to men in their relation to God, and to His law, which they had broken. These may be said to be, chiefly, so far as our present subject is concerned, reconciliation to God, —the expiation of sin, —and the redemption of sinners, — καταλλαγή, ἱλασμος, λύτρωσις. These are all ascribed in Scripture to the death of Christ; and there are two questions that naturally arise to be discussed in regard to them, though, in the very brief remarks we can make upon them, the two questions may be answered together: First, What do they mean or what is the nature of the changes effected upon men's condition which they express? Secondly, What light is cast by the nature of these changes or effects, when once ascertained, upon the true character of the death of Christ, —and more especially upon the great question, whether or not it was endured in our room and stead, and thus made satisfaction for our sins?

Reconciliation naturally and ordinarily implies that two parties, who were formerly at variance and enmity with each other, have been brought into a state of harmony and friendship; and if this reconciliation between God and man was effected, as Scripture assures us it was, by the death of Christ, then the fair inference would seem to be, that His death had removed obstacles which previously stood in the way of the existence or the manifestation of friendship between them, —had made it, in some way or other, fully accordant with the principles, the interests, or the inclinations of both parties to return to a state of friendly intercourse. We need not repeat, in order to guard against misconstruction, what was formerly explained, —in considering objections to the doctrine of the atonement founded on misrepresentations about the eternal and unchangeable love of God to men, —about the atonement being the consequence and not the cause of God's love, and about its introducing no feeling into the divine mind which did not exist there before. If this be true, as it certainly is, and if it be also true that the death of Christ is represented as propitiating God to men, —as turning away His wrath from them, —and as effecting their restoration to His favour, —then it follows plainly that it must have removed obstacles to the manifestation of His love, and opened up a channel for His actual bestowing upon them tokens of His kindness; and if these obstacles consisted in the necessity of exercising and manifesting His justice, and maintaining unimpaired the honour of His law, which men had broken, then the way or manner in which the death of Christ operated in effecting a reconciliation between God and man, must hare been by its satisfying God's justice, and answering the demands of His law. Socinians, indeed, allege that it is not said in Scripture that God was reconciled to men by the death of Christ, but only that men were reconciled to God, or that God in this way reconciled men to Himself; and that the only way in which the death of Christ operated in effecting this reconciliation, was by its affording motives and encouragements to men to repent and turn to Him. It is admitted that it is not expressly said in Scripture that the death of Christ reconciled God to men; but then it is contended, and can be easily proved, that statements of equivalent import to this occur; and more especially, that it is in accordance with Scripture usage, in the application of the word reconcile, that those who are said to be reconciled, are represented, not as laying aside their enmity against the other party, but as aiming at and succeeding in getting Him to lay aside His righteous enmity against them; and this general use of the word, applied to the case under consideration, leaves the argument for a real atonement, deduced from the asserted effect of Christ's death upon the reconciliation of God and man untouched, in all its strength and cogency.

The next leading effect ascribed to the death of Christ is that it expiates sin, as expressed by the word ἱλάσκομαι, and its derivatives. The statements in which these words occur, bring out somewhat more explicitly the effect of Christ's sufferings and death upon men's relation to God and to His law, and thus at once confirm and illustrate what is said about its bearing upon reconciliation. It can be fully established, that the true and proper meaning of these words is, to propitiate, or to make propitious one who had been righteously offended by transgression, so that the transgression is no longer regarded as a reason for manifesting o o o o displeasure or inflicting punishment. Christ is repeatedly described in Scripture as being a propitiation for sins, ἱλασμός περὶ ἁμαρτιῶν; and we are also told that His humiliation and His execution of the priestly office were directed to the object of making propitiation for, or expiating the sins of, the people. This is translated in our version, to make reconciliation for the sins of the people: but it would be more correctly rendered, to propitiate by expiating their sins. And in another passage,) where He is also described as a propitiation, — this is expressly connected with His blood as an object of faith, and with the result of the remission of sins: it being a great principle regulating God's dealings with sinners, that without tin shedding of blood then is no remission. If Christ was thus a propitiation, or propitiated God to men who had sinned against Him, and if He effected this through His humiliation and blood-shedding, it could be only by its being an atonement for their sins, or expiatory of their sins, —that is, by its presenting or affording some adequate cause or reason why the punishment of their sins should not be inflicted upon them; and this, according to every idea suggested in Scripture concerning expiation or atonement, or expiatory sacrifices, —sacrifices which, as is often said in the Old Testament, make atonement,— could be only by its being the endurance in their room and instead of the punishment they had incurred.

The general ideas expressed by some of these leading words, as descriptive of the effect of Christ's death upon men's condition and relation to God, are well stated by Dr John Pye Smith in this way: In enumerating the glorious effects of Christ's sacrifice, he specifics as one, "The legal reconciliation of God and all sinners who cordially receive the gospel method of salvation and then he adds, "This all-important idea is presented under two aspects: First, Expiation or atonement. This denotes the doing of something which shall furnish a just ground or reason in a system of judicial administration, for pardoning a convicted offender. Secondly, Propitiation: anything which shall have the property of disposing, inclining, or causing the judicial authority to admit the expiation; that is, to assent to it as a valid reason for pardoning the offender."

The third leading result ascribed to Christ's death, in its bearing upon the condition of sinners in relation to God and His law, is redemption. As we are assured in Scripture, both that Christ died fur sins and that he died for sinners, so we are told, both that sins and sinners were redeemed by Him, by His blood, by His giving Himself for them; though the idea most frequently indicated is, that, by dying for sinners, He redeemed or purchased them, he is described as giving His life, —which, of course, is the same thing as His submitting to death, —as a λύτρον, and as giving Himself as an αντίλύτρον for men. Now, there is no doubt about the true, proper, ordinary meaning of these words: λύτρον means a ransom price, —a price paid in order to secure the deliverance of a debtor or a captive; and αντίλύτρον means the same thing, with a more explicit indication, —the effect of the prefixed preposition, —of the idea of commutation, compensation, or substitution, —that is, of the price being paid in the room and stead of something else for which it is substituted. Christ's blood or death, then, is frequently and explicitly represented in Scripture as a ransom price paid by Him, in order to effect, and actually effecting, the deliverance of men from sin, and from the injurious effects of sin upon their relation to God and their eternal welfare. And if there be any truth or reality in this representation, —if anything is meant by it at all corresponding to the words in which it is conveyed to us, then it is manifest that, taken in connection with what we know from Scripture as to men's natural state or condition, and the real nature of the difficulties or obstacles that stood in the way of their deliverance, it shuts us up to the conclusion that Christ, in suffering and dying, acted in the room and stead of sinners; and by enduring, as their substitute, the punishment which they had deserved, rendered satisfaction to the justice and law of God in their behalf.

These, then, are the leading divisions under which the extensive and varied mass of Scripture evidence for the great doctrine of the atonement may be classed: first, the general character of Christ's sufferings and death, as being the offering up of Himself as a sacrifice; secondly, the true nature and immediate object of His death, as implying that he took the place of sinners, and in all His sufferings endured the punishment which they had merited; and, thirdly and finally, the bearing or effect of His death upon their relation to God and His law, —every feature and aspect of the resulting effect, or of the change produced, affording a strong confirmation of His having acted as their substitute, and rendered satisfaction to divine justice for their sins.

Chapter Six

SOCINIAN VIEW OF THE ATONEMENT

E very position laid down by the defenders of the doctrine has been controverted, and every one of them has been successfully established. It is necessary to know something, not only of the grounds of the leading scriptural positions on which this great doctrine is based, but also of the objections by which they have been assailed, and of the way in which these objections have been answered. There are, however, two or three general observations on the method commonly adopted by the Socinians in dealing with the Scripture evidence in reference to this doctrine, which it may be worth while to bring under notice.

Of course they feel it to be necessary to attempt to explain, in consistency with the denial of the atonement, the special importance ascribed in Scripture to the death of Christ, as distinguished from everything else recorded regarding Him, and the peculiarity and immediateness of the connection plainly indicated between His death and the forgiveness of men's sins. Now, the substance of what they allege upon this point really amounts to this, and to nothing more,—that though, in reality, no such special importance attached to the death of Christ, and no such peculiar and immediate connection subsisted between it and the forgiveness of sin, as the doctrine of an atonement supposes, yet that reasons can be assigned why the sacred writers might naturally enough have been led to speak of it in a way that is fitted, at first sight, to convey these impressions. This is no misrepresentation of their doctrine, but a fair statement of what it involves, as could very easily be established. Of course they are fond of enlarging upon the advantages resulting from Christ's death as an example of excellence in Him, and of love to men, and as confirming the divinity of His mission and the truth of His doctrines; while they usually come at last, in discussing this point, to the admission, that the main ground why such special importance is assigned to it in Scripture is, because it was necessary as a step to His resurrection, which was intended to be the great proof of the divinity of His mission, and thus the main ground of our faith or reliance upon what He has made known to us,—a train of thought which assumes throughout, what may be regarded as the fundamental principle of Socinianism,—namely, that the sole object of Christ's mission was to reveal and establish the will of God.

We have no interest and no inclination to underrate the importance of the death of Christ, either in itself, or as connected with His resurrection, viewed as a testimony to truth,—as a ground of faith or conviction; but we cannot admit that any view of this sort accounts fully for the very special and paramount importance which the Scripture everywhere assigns to it, and still less for the peculiar and immediate connection which it everywhere indicates as subsisting between the suffering, the death, the blood-shedding of Christ, and the forgiveness of men's sins. Dr Lant Carpenter, one of the most respectable, and, upon the whole, most candid and least offensive of modern Unitarians, after enumerating a variety of circumstances in the condition of the apostles, and in the sentiments and associations it tended to produce, which might not unnaturally have led them to represent the connection between the death of Christ and the forgiveness of sin as peculiar and immediate, though it was not so (for that is really the substance of the matter), triumphantly asks, "Can we wonder that the apostles sometimes referred to this event all the blessings of the gospel, and represented it under those figures with which their religious and national peculiarities so abundantly supplied them?"* The Unitarian position, then, upon this point, is this: Though the apostles sometimes represented the connection subsisting between the death of Christ and the blessings of salvation as peculiar and immediate, we do not believe that any such peculiar and immediate connection existed; because we can imagine some circumstances and influences that might not improbably have led them to speak in this way, without supposing that they really believed or means to teach the existence of such a connection. Our position is this: The apostles speak of the sufferings and death of Christ, and of the blessings of salvation, in such a way as is fitted, and was therefore intended, to teach us that the connection between them was peculiar and immediate, and not indirect and remote, through the intervention of the efficacy of His sufferings and death, in establishing truths and influencing our motives; and therefore we believe this upon their authority. It is surely manifest, that the only honest way of coming to a decision between these two positions, is to take up and settle the previous question,—namely, whether or not the apostles were directly commissioned to reveal the will of God? whether or not the Bible is to be received as our rule of faith?

This leads us to notice the liberal use which the Socinians make,—in distorting and perverting the statement of Scripture upon this subject,—of the allegation, that the language employed by the sacred writers is very figurative, and is not to be literally understood. This is an allegation which they make and apply very largely in their whole system of scriptural interpretation; but in regard to no subject do they make so wide and sweeping a use of it, as in dealing with the doctrine of the atonement, and more especially when they come to assail what they call "the far-fetched analogies and inaccurate reasonings" of the Epistle to the Hebrews. This topic opens up a wide field of general discussion, on which we do not mean to enter. We notice merely the abuse which they make of it, in order to guard against the impression which they labour to convey, though they do not venture formally and openly to maintain it,—namely, that an allegation that a statement is figurative or metaphorical, if admitted or proved to be in any sense or to any extent true, virtually involves in total obscurity or uncertainty the meaning or import it was intended to convey. This is really the substance of what they must maintain, in order to make their favourite allegation of any real service to their cause.

A great portion of ordinary language may be said to be in some sense figurative; and one cause of this is, that most of the words employed to describe mental states or operations are taken from material objects. But this does not prevent the language, though figurative or metaphorical, from conveying to us precise and definite ideas.* Figures are, for the most part, taken from actual resemblances or analogies; and even when the figurative use of words and phrases has not been fully established, and cannot, in consequence, be directly ascertained by the ordinary usus loquendi (though, in most languages, this is not to any considerable extent the case), still the resemblances and analogies on which the figure is founded may usually be traced, and thus the idea intended to be conveyed may be distinctly apprehended,—due care, of course, being taken to apply aright any information we may possess concerning the real nature of the subject and its actual qualities and relations. Christ is described as the Lamb of God, that taketh away the sins of the world. There is no doubt something figurative here: but there can be no doubt also that it was intended, as it is fitted, to convey to us the ideas that there is some resemblance between Christ and a lamb, and a lamb, moreover, viewed as a sacrificial victim; and that Christ exerted some influence upon the remission of the sins of men analogous to that which the sacrifice of a lamb exerted in regard to the remission of the sins to which such sacrifices had a respect. What this influence or relation in both cases was, must be learned from a fair application of all that we know concerning the nature of the case in both instances, and the specific information we have received regarding them. And the fair result of a careful and impartial examination of all the evidence bearing upon these points is this, that the language of Scripture is fitted to impress upon us the convictions,—that the sacrifice of a lamb under the Mosaic economy was really vicarious, and was really expiatory of the sins to which it had a respect,—and that the sacrifice of Christ, in like manner, was really vicarious; that is, that it was presented in the room and stead of men, and that it really expiated or atoned for their sins,—that it was offered and accepted, as furnishing an adequate ground or reason why their sins should not be punished as they had deserved.

There is a great deal said in Scripture about the sufferings and death of Christ, and their relations,—viewed both in their causes and their consequences,—to men's sins. This language is partly figurative; but, first, there is no proof or evidence that it is wholly so; and, secondly, there is no great difficulty in ascertaining, with precision and certainty, what ideas the figures, that are employed in representing and illustrating them, are fitted, and were intended, to convey. And if the statements of Scripture upon this point, viewed in combination and as a whole, were not intended to convey to us the ideas that Christ, by His sufferings and death, offered a true and real sacrifice,—that He presented it in the room and stead of men, and by doing so, suffered the punishment which they had deserved, and thereby expiated their guilt, and saved them from punishment,—then the Bible can be regarded in no other light than as a series of unintelligible riddles, fitted not to instruct, but to perplex and to mock, men.* Here, as in the case of other doctrines, Socinians argue with some plausibility only when they are dealing with single passages, or particular classes of passages, but keeping out of view, or throwing into the background, the general mass of Scripture evidence bearing upon the whole subject. When we take a conjunct view of the whole body of Scripture statements, manifestly intended to make known to us the nature, causes, and consequences of Christ's death, literal and figurative,—view them in combination with each other,—and fairly estimate what they are fitted to teach, there is no good ground for doubt as to the general conclusions which we should feel ourselves constrained to adopt.

The evidence in support of the expiatory and vicarious character of Christ's death, is not only peculiarly varied and abundant; but we have, in this case, peculiar advantages for ascertaining the truth as to its intended import, in the special means we possess of knowing how the statements of the apostles would be, in point of fact, understood by those to whom they were originally addressed. We must, of course, believe that the apostles used language fitted and intended to be understood by those whom they addressed,—not accommodated to their errors and prejudices, in accordance with what is usually called the theory of accommodation; for this, integrity, not to speak of inspiration, precludes,—but fitted to convey correct impressions, if understood in the sense in which they must have known that it would be understood,—for this integrity requires. And it can be easily proved that both The Jews and the Gentiles, with the notions they generally entertained about sacrifices,—their nature, object, and effects,—must have understood the apostolic statements about Christ's sacrifice of Himself, just as they have been generally understood ever since by the great body of the Christian church. It is, then, a mere evasion of the argument, to dispose of such a body of proof by the vague allegation of the language being figurative or metaphorical, as if it could be shown that all the scriptural statements upon the subject are figurative; and, further, that the figures employed convey no meaning whatever,—or a meaning which cannot be fully ascertained,—or a meaning different from that assigned to them by the defenders of the atonement. Not only can none of these positions be proved, but all of them can be disproved; and, therefore, the evidence for this great and fundamental doctrine stands untouched and unassailable.*

There is only one of the more specific methods adopted by Socinians to evade and pervert the testimony of Scripture upon this subject to which I shall particularly advert; but it is one of pretty extensive application. It may be described, in general, as consisting in this,—that they labour to show that most of the scriptural statements about the suffering and death of Christ are descriptive merely of certain results, without indicating anything of the means, or intermediate process, by which the results are effected. This will be best understood by giving two or three examples. With reference to the connection between the sin of man and the death of Christ, in its causes, they usually maintain that sin was only the final cause of Christ's death,—in no proper sense its impulsive, procuring cause, and in no sense whatever its meritorious cause. By sin being the final cause of Christ's death, they mean that it was the end or object of His death to save men from sin,—which is certainly true; but then they deny that we have any further information given us in Scripture respecting any causal connection between our sin and Christ's death: while we contend that the scriptural representations warrant us in asserting, not only that Christ died in order to save men from sin, but, further, that man's sin was the procuring cause of His death,—that which rendered His death necessary, and really brought it to pass,—and did so by meriting or deserving that we should die. Christ's dying for sinners, according to the Socinians, means merely His dying for their sates, on their account,—for their good,—in order to benefit them. This we admit to be true,—to be implied in the scriptural statements the upon subject; but we contend, further, that these statements, in their genuine import, teach that He died in our room and stead, and that by dying in our room and stead as the means. He effected our good as the result. Bearing sin, according to the Socinians, means merely taking it away or removing it, and is thus descriptive merely of the result of His interposition,—in that, in consequence, men are not actually subjected to what their sin deserved; whereas we contend that its true and proper meaning is, that He assumed or had laid upon Him the guilt, or legal answerableness, or legal liability to punishment, on account of our sins, and endured this punishment; and that by thus bearing our sin as a means, He effected the end or result of bearing it away or removing it, so that it no longer lies upon us, to subject us to punishment. According to our view of the import of the expression, it implies that our sin was on Christ,—was laid on Him,—and that thus He bore it, in order to bear it away; whereas, on the Socinian interpretation, our sin never was on Him, and He bore it away, or accomplished the result of freeing us from the effects of it, without ever having borne it. Redemption, according to the Socinians, just means deliverance as an end aimed at, and result effected, without indicating anything as to the means by which it was accomplished; and it is not disputed that, in some instances, the word redeem is used in this wide and general sense. But we contend that its proper ordinary meaning is to effect deliverance as an end, through the means of a price or ransom paid: and we undertake to show, not only from the proper ordinary meaning of the word itself,—from which there is no sufficient reason for deviating,—but from the whole connections in which it occurs, and especially the specification of the actual price or ransom paid, that it ought, in its application to the death of Christ, to be understood as descriptive of the means by which the result of deliverance is effected, as well as the actual deliverance itself. Of course, in each case the question as to the true meaning of the statements must be determined by a diligent and impartial application of philological and critical rules material; but this brief statement of these distinctions may perhaps be of some use in explaining the true state of the question upon the Scripture evidence,—in guarding against Socinian sophisms and evasions,—and in indicating what are some of the leading points to be attended to in the investigation of this subject.

CHAPTER SEVEN

ARMINIAN VIEW
OF THE
ATONEMENT

I n introducing the subject of atonement, I proposed to consider, first, the reality and general nature of the vicarious atonement or satisfaction of Christ, as it has been generally held by the Christian church in opposition to the Socinians; secondly, the peculiarities of the doctrine commonly held by Arminians upon this subject, as connected with the other leading features of their scheme of theology; and, thirdly, the peculiar views of those who hold Calvinistic doctrines upon most other points, but upon this concur with, or approximate to, the views of the Arminians. The first of these topics I have already examined; I now proceed to advert to the second,—namely, the peculiarities of the Arminian doctrine upon the subject of the atonement or satisfaction of Christ. I do not mean, however, to dwell at any great length upon this second head, because most of the topics that might be discussed under it recur again, with some modifications, under the third head; and as they are more dangerous there, because of the large amount of truth in connection with which they are held, I propose then to consider them somewhat more fully.

The leading peculiarity of the doctrine of the Arminians upon this subject is usually regarded as consisting in this,—that they believe in a universal or unlimited atonement, or teach that Christ died and offered up an expiatory sacrifice for the sins of all men,—that is, of all the individuals of the human race, without distinction or exception. This doctrine was the subject of the second of the five articles,—the first being on predestination,—which were discussed and condemned in the Synod of Dort. Their leading tenets upon this subject, as give in to the Synod of Dort, and condemned there, were these,—first, that the price of redemption, which Christ offered to His Father, is not only in and of itself sufficient for redeeming the whole human race, but that, according to the decree, the will, and the grace of God the Father, it was actually paid for all and every man; and, secondly, that Christ, by the merit of His death, has so far reconciled God His Father to the whole human race, as that the Father, on account of His merit, was able, consistently with His justice and veracity, and actually willed or resolved, to enter into a new covenant of grace with sinful men exposed to condemnation. Now, these statements, it will be observed, direct our thoughts, not only to the extent, but also to the nature, the objects, and the effects of the atonement, or of the payment of the reason price of men's deliverance and salvation. Their doctrine upon both these points was also comprehended by themselves in one proposition in this way: "Christ died for all and every man, and did so in this sense and to this effect,—that He obtained, or procured (imperative), for all men by His death reconciliation and the forgiveness of their sins; but upon this condition, that none actually possess and enjoy this forgiveness of sins except believers."* The substance of the doctrine is this,—first, that Christ's death, in the purpose of God and in His own intention in submitting to it, was directed to the benefit of all men, equally and alike; secondly, that its only proper and direct effect was to enable and incline God to enter into a new covenant with them upon more favourable terms than, but for Christ's dying for them, would have been granted; and that this is virtually the same thing as His procuring or obtaining for all men reconciliation with God and the forgiveness of their sins.

Now, this is plainly a scheme of doctrine which is throughout consistent with itself. And more especially it is manifest, that, if the atonement was universal or unlimited,—if it was intended to benefit all men,—its proper nature and immediate object must have been, in substance, just what the Arminians represent it to have been; or, more generally, the doctrine of the universality of the atonement must materially affect men's views of its nature and immediate object. Arminians generally concur with other sections of the Christian church in maintaining the doctrine of a vicarious and expiatory atonement, in opposition to the socinians; and of course they defend the general ideas of substitution and satisfaction,—that is, of Christ's having put Himself in our place, and satisfied divine justice in our room and stead; but when they come more minutely and particularly to explain what substitution and satisfaction mean, and in what way the atonement of Christ is connected with, and bears upon, the forgiveness and salvation of men individually, then differences of no small importance come out between them and those who have more scriptural views of the scheme of divine truth in general, and then is manifested a considerable tendency on their part to dilute or explain away what seems to be the natural import of the terms commonly employed in relation to this matter. It may not be easy to determine whether their doctrine of the universality of the atonement produced their modified and indefinite views of its proper nature and immediate object, or whether certain defective and erroneous view upon this latter point led them to assert its universality. But certain it is, that their doctrine with respect to its nature, and their doctrine with respect to its extent, are intimately connected together,—the one naturally leading to and producing the other. As the doctrine of the universality of the atonement professes to be founded upon, and derived from, Scripture statements directly bearing upon the point, and is certainly not destitute of an appearance of Scripture support, the probability is, that this was the πρωτον ψεῦδος,—the primary or originating error,—which produced their erroneous views in regard to the nature and immediate object of the atonement. And this is confirmed by the fact, that the ablest Arminian writers, such as Curcellæas and Limborch,* have been accustomed to urge the universality of the atonement as a distinct and independent argument against the Calvinistic doctrine of election,—that it, they undertake to prove directly from Scripture that Christ died for all men; and then, having proved this, they draw from in the inference that it was impossible that there could have been from eternity an election of some men to life, and a reprobation, or preterition, or passing by of others,—an argument which, it appears to me, the Calvinistic defenders of an unlimited atonement are not well able to grapple with.

But whatever may have been the state of this matter historically, it is quite plain that there is, and must be, a very close connection between men's views with regard to the nature and immediate object and effect, and with regard to the extent, of the atonement. If Christ died and gave Himself for those who, in point of fact, are never pardoned, sanctified, and saved, the object and immediate effects of His submitting to death must be very different from what they at least may be, if His sacrifice was offered and accepted only for those who are ultimately saved. The nature of His sacrifice, and the whole of the relation in which it stands to spiritual blessings and eternal life, must, in the one case, be essentially different from what it may be in the other. We think it of some importance to illustrate this position; and therefore,—reserving the consideration of the alleged universality of the atonement, as a distinct and independent topic, till we come to the third head of our proposed division of the whole subject,—we will now attempt to explain some of the peculiar view, usually held more or less explicitly by Arminians, in regard to the nature, object, and immediate effects of the atonement, as illustrative of the tendency and results of their doctrine of its universality; remarking, however, that a very considerable difference of sentiment upon this subject,—and, indeed, in regard to some other fundamental doctrines of Christianity, such as original sin and regeneration by the Holy Spirit,—prevails among those who may be classed under the general head of Arminians, because they all deny what are called the peculiarities of Calvinism; and that the representations about to be made apply, in their full extent, only to the more Pelagian Arminians.

First, it is very common among Arminians to deny what orthodox divines have generally contended for, as we have explained, under the head of the necessity of an atonement. The reason of this must be sufficiently manifest from what has already been said upon this subject, especially in illustrating the connection between the necessity of an atonement, and its true nature, as implying substitution and satisfaction. If an atonement was not necessary, because God's perfections, moral government, and law required it is a preliminary to pardon or forgiveness, then any provision—no matter what might be its proper nature and peculiar character—might serve the purpose, might be sufficient for accomplishing the intended object; and, of course, substitution and satisfaction might not be required, excepting only in some very vague and indefinite sense, that might admit to a large extent of being modified or explained away. Still Arminians commonly admit, in a general sense, what the Socinians deny,—namely, that the divine perfections, government, and law did interpose obstacles in the way of the forgiveness and acceptance of sinners, and that these obstacles the atonement of Christ has removed or taken out of the way; while some of them maintain the necessity of an atonement upon ground similar to those laid down by orthodox divines. Secondly, many Arminians deny that Christ's sufferings and death were a properly penal infliction, and that He endured the penalty due to men's sins; or, at least, have great scruples about the propriety of describing it by this language. They admit, of course, that He suffered something in our room and stead, and if they did not, they would wholly concur with the Socinians; but they commonly, at least in modern times, deny either, first, that what He suffered was properly punishment or, secondly, that it was the same as, or equivalent to, the penalty which men had deserved by their transgressions. These notions plainly indicate a disposition to modify and explain away the real import of scriptural statements, and involve a descent to the very borders of Socinianism. If Christ suffered at all as our substitute,—if He suffered in our room and stead,—than it is manifest, that, must have been penal; that is, it must have been inflicted judicially, in the execution of the provisions of a law which demanded punishment against men's sins. And, as we formerly explained, it is mere trifling to attempt, as is often done, to settle this question about the penalty of Christ's sufferings, by laying down beforehand a definition of punishment, which includes in it, as a constituent element, personal demerit, or a consciousness of personal demerit, on the part of the individual suffering.

The most important question, however, connected with this department of the subject, is not whether what Christ suffered was a punishment, or properly penal, but whether it was the penalty which the law had denounced against sin, and to which sinners, therefore, are justly exposed. Now, upon this point, there are three different modes of statement which have been adopted and defended by different classes of divines, who all concur in maintaining the doctrine of the atonement against the Socinians. Some contend that the only accurate and exact way of expressing and embodying the doctrine of Scripture upon the subject, is to say, that Christ suffered the very penalty—the same thing viewed legally and judicially—which the law had denounced against sin, and which we had incurred by transgression. Others think that the full import of the Scripture doctrine is expressed, and that the general scope and spirit of its statements upon this subject are more accurately conveyed, by maintaining that Christ did not suffer the very penalty,—the same penalty which sinners had incurred,—but that He suffered what was a full equivalent, or an adequate compensation for it,—that His suffering was virtually as much as men deserved, though not the same. While others, again, object to both these statements, and think that the whole of what Scripture teaches upon this point is embodied in the position, that what Christ suffered was a substitute for the penalty which we had incurred.

Dr Owen zealously contends for the first of these positions, and attaches much importance to the distinction between Christ having suffered or paid the same penalty as we had incurred, and His having suffered or paid only an equivalent, or as much as we had deserved; or, as he expresses it, between His suffering or paying the idem and the tantundem. He lays down the doctrine which he maintained upon this point against Grotius and Baxter in this way: "That the punishment which our Saviour underwent was the same that the law required of us; God relaxing His law as to the persons suffering, but not as to the penalty

suffered."* There are, however, divines of the strictest orthodoxy, and
of the highest eminence, who have not attached the same importance
to the distinction between the idem and the tantundem, and who have
though that the true import of the Scripture doctrine upon the subject
is most correctly brought out by saying, that what Christ suffered was a
full equivalent, or an adequate compensation, for the penalty men had
incurred. Mastricht, for instance, whose system of theology is eminent-
ly distinguished for its ability, clearness, and accuracy, formally argues
against the death of Christ being solutio "proprie sic dieta, qua id præcise
præstatur, quod est in obligatione;" and contends that "reatus tollitur
satisfactione, qua non idem præcise, quod est in obligatione, creditori
præstatur; sed tantundem, sen equivalens." And Turretine seems, upon
the whole, to agree with him, or rather, to conjoin the two ideas together,
as being both true, though in somewhat different respects, and as not
essentially differing from each other. He has not, indeed, so far as I
remember, formally discussed the precise question about the idem and
the tantundem, on which Owen and Mastricht have taken opposite side;
but in discussing the Socinian argument,—that Christ did not make a
true and real satisfaction for our sins, because He did not in fact pay what
was due to God by us, and especially because He suffered only temporal,
while we had incurred eternal, death,—he meets the major proposition
by asserting that there might be a true and proper satisfaction, though
the same thing was not paid which was due, provided it was a full equivalent in weight and value, "etsi non idem, modo tantundem habeatur,
sufficit;" while he meets also the minor proposition of the Socinian argument, by asserting that Christ did pay what was due by us; the same, not
of course in its adjuncts and circumstances, but in its substance,—His
suffering, though temporary in duration, being, because of the infinite
dignity of His person, properly infinite in weight or value as a penal

infliction, and thus substantially identical, in the eye of justice and law, with the eternal punishment which sinners had deserved.

The difference, then, between the idem and the tantundem in this matter does not seem to be quite so important as Dr Owen believed. The difference between the temporary suffering of on being and the eternal sufferings of millions of other beings, is so great, as to their outward aspects and adjuncts, or accompanying circumstances, as to make it not very unreasonable that men should hesitate about calling them the same thing. And the Scripture doctrine of the substitution and satisfaction of Christ seems to be fully brought out, if His death be represented as a full equivalent or an adequate compensation for the sins of men,—as being not only a penal infliction, but an infliction of such weight and value intrinsically, as to be a real and full compliance with the demands of the law denouncing death against sin; and thus to exhaust in substance the position which Scripture plainly teachers,—namely, that He bore our sins,—that is, that He suffered the punishment which we had deserved, and must otherwise have borne. The danger of admitting that Christ suffered the tantundem, and not the idem,—an equivalent or compensation, ad not the same thing which we had deserved,—lies here, that men are very apt to dilute or explain away the idea of equivalency or compensation, and to reduce it to anything or nothing; and experience has fully illustrated this tendency. The sounder Arminians have usually admitted that Christ's death was an equivalent or compensation for men's sins; but they have generally scrupled, or refused to call it a full equivalent,—an adequate compensation. The reason of this is obvious enough; for this latter idea naturally suggests, that is must be certainly effectual for all its intended objects,—that it must be part of a great scheme, fitted and designed to accomplish certain definite results; whereas, under the more vague and general idea of mere equivalency or compensation, which may be understood in a very wide sense, they can, with some plausibility, retain their nations of its universality, its indefiniteness, and its unsettled and uncertain application. Accordingly, in modern times, they have usually rejected even the idea of equivalency in any proper sense, and adopted the third of the positions formerly mentioned,—namely, that Christ neither suffered the same penalty which we had deserved, nor what was an equivalent for it, but merely what was a substitute for the penalty. This idea leaves them abundant scope for diluting or attenuating, to any extent, the substitution and satisfaction which they still continue, in words, to ascribe to Christ. And, accordingly, it is usually adopted by most of those, in our own day,—whether Arminians or professing Calvinists in other respects,—who hold the doctrine of a universal or unlimited atonement.

The word equivalent, when honestly used, naturally suggested the idea, not indeed of precise identity, but still of substantial sameness, at least of adequacy or competency, when tried by some definite and understood standard, to serve the same purposes, or to effect the same objects; whereas a substitute for the penalty may be almost anything whatever. A substitute may, indeed, be an equivalent, even a full equivalent, or anything short of, or different from, what is precisely identical; but it may also and equally describe something of which nothing like equivalency or substantial identity can be predicated. And hence the danger, to which I formerly referred, as apprehended by Dr Owen and others, of departing from the idea and the phraseology of strict and precise identity. If it was not the same thing, it must have been a substitute for it; and as even a full equivalent, which implies substantial identity, may be classed under the general name of substitute, men's ideas are thus gradually and imperceptibly lowered, until at length by the dexterous use of vague and indefinite language, they are cheated out of very distinct and definite conceptions of the real nature of Christ's death, in its relation to the law which they had broken, and which He magnified and made honourable by fulfilling all its demands,—being made a curse, in our room, that He might redeem us from the curse of the law.

This idea of Christ having suffered, not the penalty we had deserved and incurred nor an equivalent for it, but merely a substitute for it,—that is, anything which God might choose to accept instead of it, without there being any standard by which its adequacy for its professed object could be tried or tested,—has been much dwelt upon, in the present day, by the advocates of a universal atonement, even among those who disclaim Arminianism in other respects. It is, however, an Arminian notion; nay, it is disclaimed by many of the sounder Arminians, and has been generally and justly regarded by Calvinists as amounting to what is practically little else than a denial of the atonement altogether. Limborch, in explaining the doctrine of the Arminians upon this subject, which he represents as the golden mean between the Socinian and the Calvinistic views, makes the difference between them to consist chiefly in this, that Calvinists represented Christ as suffering the same penalty which men had deserved, or a full equivalent for it, which, of course, implies substantial sameness; while Arminians regarded Him as merely suffering something or other for them, which might serve as a substitute for the penalty, and might stand "vice pœnæ," as he says, in the room or stead of the penalty. He felt, however, that this might very probably be regarded as amounting to a virtual denial that Christ had suffered, or been punished, in our room, and thus as approximating to Socinianism; and, accordingly, he proposes this objection to his own doctrine, and answers it, "An non ergo nostro loco punitus est?" And his answer is this, "Eadem quam nos meriti eramus specie pœnæ non punitum esse jam osteudinius,"—a statement plainly implying an admission of what indeed

is manifestly undeniable,—namely, that the natural, obvious meaning of
His suffering punishment in our room is, that He endured, either literally and precisely, or at least substantially and equivalently, the penalty
which we had incurred; and that this must be held to be its meaning,
unless it could be proved, as he professed it had been, to be false. And
then he adds, "Potest tamen certo sensu pro nobis dici punitus, quatenus
pœnam vicariam, pro beneplacito divino sibi imponendam, hoc est,
afflictionem, quæ pœnæ vicem sustinuit, in se suscepit."* This sense of
pœna vicaria,—as meaning, not a punishment endured in the room and
stead of others who had deserved it, but merely suffering endured, vice
pœnœ, in the room of punishment, or as a substitute for the penalty,—is
fully adopted by the modern defenders of universal atonement, Beman,
Jenkyn, etc.

We insist, of course, that the Scripture statements about the connection between our sin and our pardon on the one hand, and the death
of Christ on the other, are not fully accounted for,—are not sufficiently
explained and exhausted,—by the position that Christ suffered something, which might be called a substitute for the penalty, and which God
might choose to accept instead of it; and that they are to be taken in
what Limborch, by plain implication, admits, and no one can deny, to
be their natural, ordinary meaning, as importing that He had inflicted
upon Him, and actually endured, what may be fairly and honestly called
the penalty we had deserved and incurred. Limborch rejects this interpretation, because he thinks he has proved that it is not accordant with
the facts of the case; that is, that, in fact, Christ did not suffer the penalty
which the law had denounced against us. His proofs are these: First, that
Christ did not suffer eternal death, which was what we had merited by
transgression; and, secondly, that if He had suffered the penalty, or a
full equivalent, in our room, there would be no grace or gratuitousness

on God's part in forgiving men's sins. The last of these arguments we have already considered and refuted, when we mentioned that it was commonly adduced, not only by Socinians, against satisfaction in any sense, but also by the advocates of universal atonement, in opposition to those more strict and proper views of the nature of substitution and satisfaction, which are plainly inconsistent with their doctrine. And there is no more weight in the other argument, that Christ's sufferings were only temporary, while those we had incurred by sin were eternal. This may be, as we have already intimated, a good reason for adopting the phraseology of full equivalency, instead of precise identity,—the tantundem instead of the idem. But it furnishes no disproof of substantial sameness, viewed with reference to the demands of law. The law denounced and demanded death, and Christ died for us. The law denounced eternal suffering against an innumerable multitude, who are, in fact, saved from ruin, and admitted to everlasting blessedness. But the temporary suffering and death, in human nature, of One who was at the same time a possessor of the divine nature, was, in point of weight and value, as a compliance with the provisions of the law, a satisfaction to its demands, a testimony to its infinite excellence and unchangeable obligation, a full equivalent for all.

I have dwelt the longer upon this point, because the views which, as we have seen, were held by the more Pelagian or Socinianizing portion of the Arminians,—as they are often called by the orthodox divines of the seventeenth century,—are the very same in substance as those which, in the present day, are advocated, more or less openly, even by the Calvinistic defenders of a universal atonement. They involve, I think, a most unwarrantable dilution or explaining away of the true meaning of the scriptural statements concerning the nature, causes, and objects of Christ's death; and in place of occupying the golden mean between the Socinian and the true Calvinistic doctrines, make a decided approximation to the former. It may be proper to mention, before leaving this topic, that this Arminian notion of the sufferings and death of Christ being merely a substitute for the penalty which sinners had deserved,—as implying something less than an equivalent or compensation, or at least than a full equivalent, an adequate compensation,—is commonly discussed by orthodox divines, under the name of acceptilatio,—a law term, which is employed to express a nominal, fictitious, or illusory payment.*

A third peculiarity of the opinions commonly held by Arminians on this subject is, that they regard the appointment and acceptance of Christ's satisfaction as involving a relaxation or virtual abrogation of the divine law. This necessarily follows from what has been already explained. As Christ did not suffer the penalty of the law, or a full equivalent for it, but only a substitute for the penalty,—which God, of His good pleasure, agreed to accept, in the room or stead of the endurance of it by sinners who had incurred it,—the law was in no sense executed or enforced, but was virtually abrogated or set aside; whereas orthodox divines contend that the law was executed or enforced, the penalty which it denounced having been endured. It is of great importance, in order to our right understanding of the whole scheme of divine truth, that we should have correct conceptions and impressions of the perfection and unchangeableness of the law which God originally gave to man; as this doctrine, when rightly applied, tends equally to exclude the opposite extremes of Neonomianism, which is a necessary constituent element of Arminianism, and of Antinomianism, which is only an abuse or perversion of Calvinism, and for which Calvinism is in no way responsible. It is very easy to prove, as general doctrine, that the moral law, as originally given by God to man, was, and must have been, perfect in its nature and requirements, and unchangeable in its obligations: and that God could never thereafter, without denying Himself, do anything which fairly implied, or was fitted to convey, the impression, that this law was defective in any respect,—was too rigid in its requirements, or too severe in its sanctions, or could stand in need either of derogation or abrogation. And yet the denial or disregard of this important principle,—which indeed is, and can be, fully admitted and applied only by Calvinists,—is at the root of much of the error that prevails in some important departments of theology.

If the penalty of the law, which men had incurred, was not endured, while yet sinners were pardoned and saved, then the law was not honoured, but trampled on, in their salvation, and is thus proved to have been defective and mutable. Calvinists, of course, admit, that in the pardon of sinners there does take place what may be called, in a wide and improper sense, a relaxation of the law; since the penalty is not, in fact, inflicted upon those who had transgressed, but upon another; that is, they admit a relaxation in regard to the persons suffering, but not in regard to the penalty threatened and suffered. This is, indeed, the grand peculiarity,—the mysterious, but most glorious peculiarity, of the Christian scheme,—that which may be said to constitute the doctrine of the atonement or satisfaction of Christ, that a substitute was provided, and that His substitution was accepted. But there is nothing in this which casts any dishonour upon the law, or appears to convict it of imperfection and mutability. On the contrary, it is in every way fitted to impress upon us its absolute perfection and unchangeable obligation. In no proper sense does it involve a relaxation or abrogation of the law. The relaxation or abrogation of a law is opposed to, and precludes, compliance or fulfilment; whereas here there is compliance or fulfilment, as to the essence or substance of the matter,—namely, the infliction and endurance of the penalty, or, what is virtually the same thing, a full equivalent, an adequate compensation for it, and a relaxation only in regard to a circumstance or adjunct, namely, the particular person or persons who suffer it.

If an atonement or satisfaction be denied, then the law is wholly abrogated or set aside, and, of course, is dishonoured, by being convicted of imperfection and mutability in the salvation of sinners. And even when the idea of atonement or satisfaction is in some sense admitted, there is no real respect or honour shown to the law, because no compliance, in any fair and honest sense, with its demands,—no fulfilment of its exactions,—nothing to give us any impression of its perfection and unchangeableness in its general character, tendency, and object, unless this atonement or satisfaction was really the endurance of the penalty which the law denounced, or a full equivalent for it,—something which could serve the same purposes, with reference to the great ends of law and moral government, by impressing the same views of God's character, of His law, of sin, and of the principles that regulate His dealings with His creatures, as the actual punishment of all who had offended. Many of the human race perish, and are subjected to everlasting misery; and in them, of course, the law which denounced death as the punishment of sin, is enforced and executed. The rest are pardoned, and saved. But in their case, too, the law is not abrogated, but executed; because the penalty which they had incurred is inflicted and suffered,—is borne, not indeed by them, in their own persons, but by another, acting as their substitute, and suffering in their room and stead. The provision of a substitute, who should endure the penalty due by those who were to be pardoned and saved, is a great, glorious, and mysterious act of extra-legal mercy and compassion; it is that marvellous provision, by which sinners are saved, in consistency with the perfections of God and the principles of His moral government. But in every other step in the process, the law is enforced, and its provisions are fully complied with; for the work of the

Substitute is accepted as an adequate ground for pardoning and saving those for whom He acted, just because it was the endurance of what they had deserved,—of all that the law did or could demand of them. And in this way we see, and should ever contemplate with adoring and grateful wonder, not an abrogation or relaxation, but an execution and enforcement of the law, even in the forgiveness and salvation of those who had broken its requirements, and became subject to its curse.*

A fourth peculiarity of the views of the Arminians upon the subject of the atonement is this, that they represent its leading, proper, direct effect to be, to enable God, consistently with His justice and veracity, to enter into a new covenant with men, in which more favourable terms are proposed to them than before, and under which pardon and reconciliation are conveyed to all men conditionally,—upon the conditions of faith and repentance,—conditions which they are able to fulfil. This doctrine—which is, in substance, what is commonly called Neonomianism, or the scheme which represents the gospel as a new or modified law, offering pardon and eternal life to all men upon lower or easier terms—rests upon, as its basis, and requires for its full exposition, a more complete view of the Arminian scheme of theology, than merely their doctrine upon the subject of the atonement. It involves, of course, a denial of the scriptural and Calvinistic doctrines of predestination, and of the entire depravity of human nature; but we have to do with it at present in a more limited aspect, as a part of their doctrine of the atonement. And here, the substance of the charge which we adduce against it is just this,—that, like the doctrine of the Socinians, it explains away the true and fair import of the scriptural statements with respect to the nature of the connection between the sacrificial death of Christ and the forgiveness of men's sins, and represents that connection as much more remote and indirect than the Scripture does. It is true that the Scripture represents

Christ, by His death, as ratifying and sealing a new and better covenant, of which He was the Surety or Sponsor; but then this covenant was not based upon the abrogation or relaxation of the original law, and the introduction of a new one, which offered life upon easier terms,—upon more favourable conditions, as the Arminian scheme represents the matter. On the contrary, as we have seen, it implied that the original law was enforced and executed; Christ, as the Surety or Sponsor of His people, fulfilling the conditions of this new covenant, just by complying with the demand of the original law—by enduring, in their room and stead, the penalty which it denounced. The Scripture represents, not only the ultimate object, but the direct and immediate effect, of Christ's sacrifice of Himself, to be to save sinners,—that is, to effect, procure, provide everything which their salvation implies or requires,—everything which is Necessary to accomplish it; whereas, upon the Arminian theory, the salvation of sinners, as an actual results, was only the ultimate object of His death, its immediate effect being merely, as they are accustomed to express it, to make men—all men—salvable, or capable of being saved, and not to save them, or to secure their salvation. His death, upon their system, really effected nothing, but only enabled God to do thereafter whatever He pleased, in the way of conferring—upon any conditions which He might now think proper to require—forgiveness, acceptance, and eternal life. Accordingly, they are accustomed to describe its immediate object and effect as being merely this,—that it removed legal obstacles, and opened a door to God's bestowing, and men's receiving, pardon and salvation; and they consider it as effecting this, not because it was a compliance with the demands of the law, in the room and stead of those who were to be benefited by it, but merely became it was a great display of hatred to sin and of love to righteousness; after having made which, God could safely, or without any danger of conveying erroneous impressions of His character, bestow pardon and spiritual blessings upon all alike who were willing to accept of them.

This representation is in substance true, so far as it goes; but, like the common Socinian doctrine, it falls short of embodying the whole truth which Scripture teaches upon the subject, and of bringing it out so fully and distinctly as Scripture affords us materials for doing. We are not told in Scripture that Christ's death removed legal obstacles, and opened a door for men's pardon and salvation: but we admit that the statements are true—that the death of Christ did this, because it seems fairly involved in, or deducible from, the scriptural statements which warrant us in believing the more precise and definite doctrine,—that, by dying in our room, Christ satisfied the divine justice and law, and thereby reconciled us to God. There were obstacles in the way of God's bestowing upon men pardon and salvation, and these required to be removed; the door was shut, and it needed to be opened. From the position which the death of Christ occupied in the scheme of salvation, and from the general effects ascribed to it, we feel that we are fully warranted in representing it as removing the obstacles and opening the door. But we contend that this does not by any means exhaust the Scripture account of its proper objects and effects, which represents it as more directly and immediately efficacious in accomplishing men's redemption from sin, and their enjoyment of God's favour. The Scripture not only indicates a closer and more direct connection as subsisting between the death of Christ and the actual pardon and salvation of men than the Arminian doctrine admits of; but it also, as we have seen, explains the connection between its proper nature and its immediate object and effect, by setting it before us, not merely as a display of the principles of the divine government and law,—although it was this,—but, more distinctly and precisely, as the endurance of the penalty of the law in our room. It was just because it was the endurance of the penalty,—or, what is virtually the same thing, of a full equivalent for it,—that it was, or could be, a display or manifestation of the principles of the divine government and love; and it bore upon the pardon and salvation of men, not merely through the intervention of its being such a display or manifestation,—though this consideration is true, and is not to be overlooked,—but still more directly from its own proper nature, as being a penal infliction, in accordance with the provisions of the law, endured in our room and stead, and as thus furnishing an adequate ground or reason why those in whose room it was suffered should not suffer, in their own person, the penalty which they had incurred.

The Arminians, holding the universality of the atonement, and rejecting the doctrine of election, regard the death of Christ as equally fitted, and equally intended, to promote the spiritual welfare and eternal salvation of all men; and, of course, cannot but regard it as very indirectly and remotely connected with the results to which it was directed. Of those for whom Christ died, for whose salvation His death was intended,—that is, of the whole human race,—some are saved, and some perish. If He died for all equally, for both classes alike, His death cannot be the proper cause or ground of the salvation of any, and can have no direct or efficacious connection with salvation in any instance; and hence it is quite consistent in Arminians to represent the proper and immediate effect of His death to be merely that of enabling God, safely and honourably, to pardon any man who complied with the conditions He prescribed, or, what is virtually the same thing, that of procuring for Christ Himself the power of bestowing pardon upon any who might choose to accept of it;—that, merely, of removing obstacles, or opening a door, without containing or producing any provision for effecting or securing that any men should enter in at the door, and actually partake of the blessings of salvation provided for them.

The general doctrine of the Arminians, with regard to the immediate object and effect of Christ's death being merely to enable God to pardon any who might be willing to accept the boon,—to remove out of the way legal obstacles to any or all men being pardoned,—to open a door into which any who choose might enter, and, by entering, obtain reconciliation and forgiveness,—is usually brought out more fully and distinctly in the way of maintaining the two following positions: First, that the impetration and the application of reconciliation and pardon, are not only distinct in idea or conception, but separate or disjoined in fact or reality; and, secondly,—what is virtually the same general principle, more distinctly developed, or an immediate consequence of it,—that while a causal or meritorious connection, though not direct and immediate, subsists between the death of Christ and the pardon of men's sins, no causal or meritorious connection exists between the death of Christ and faith and repentance, without which, no man is actually reconciled to God, or forgiven; and to these two positions we would briefly advert.

First, They teach that Christ, by His sufferings and death, impetrated or procured pardon and reconciliation for men—for all men,—meaning thereby nothing more, in substance, than that He removed legal obstacles, and opened a door for God bestowing pardon and reconciliation upon all who would accept of them; while they also teach, that to many for whom these blessings were thus impetrated or procured by Him, even to all who ultimately perish, these blessings are not in fact applied. The reason,—the sole reason,—why these men do not actually partake in the blessings thus procured for them, is, because they refuse to do what is in their own power, in the way of receiving them, or complying with the prescribed conditions. But this last consideration properly belongs to another branch of the Arminian system,—namely, their denial of man's total depravity, and their assertion of his ability to repent and believe. We have at present to do with their doctrine of the possible, and actual, separation and disjunction of the impetration and the application of pardon or forgiveness. Calvinists admit that the impetration and the application of the blessings of salvation are distinct things, which may be conceived and spoken of apart from each other, which are effected by different agencies and at different periods. The impetration of all these blessings they ascribe to Christ, to what He did and suffered in our room and stead. The application of them, by which men individually become partakes in them, they ascribe to the Holy Spirit. It is the clear and constant doctrine of Scripture, that no man is actually pardoned and reconciled to God until he repent and believe. It is then only that he becomes a partaker of the blessings which Christ purchased. It is admitted, in this way, that the impetration or purchase, and the application or bestowed upon men individually, of pardon and reconciliation, are perfectly distinct from each other; but in opposition to the Arminian doctrine, which represents them as separable, and, in fact, separated and disjoined, as to the persons who are the objects of them, there is an important scriptural truth, held by almost all Calvinists,—that is, by all of them except those who believe in a universal or unlimited atonement,—which is thus stated in our Confession of Faith:* "To all those for whom Christ hath purchased redemption, He doth certainly and effectually apply and communicate the same." The word redemption is here evidently used, as it often is in Scripture, as comprehending those blessings which it was the direct object of Christ's death to procure; and it includes, of course, reconciliation with God and the forgiveness of sin. The doctrine of Scripture and of out Confession is, that to all for whom these blessings were purchased or impetrated, they are also applied or communicated; so that they all, in fact, receive and partake of them, or are actually pardoned and reconciled.

The doctrine of the Arminians is, that redemption, at least in so far as it includes the blessings of pardon and reconciliation, was procured for all men,—and for all men equally and alike; but that there are many, even all those who ultimately perish, to whom these blessings, though procured for them, are not applied or communicated,—who never, in fact, receive or partake of them. That pardon and reconciliation are not applied or communicated to many, is not a matter of dispute; this is admitted on all hands. The question is, whether they were procured, or impetrated, or purchased, for any to whom they are not applied,—for any but those to whom they are communicated, so that they actually receive, possess, and enjoy them? This, indeed, constitutes the true and correct status quæstion, with respect to the extent of the atonement. The settlement of that controversy depends upon the decision of this question,—whether or not Christ impetrated, or procured, or purchased reconciliation and pardon for any men expect those to whom these blessings are actually applied,—are ultimately communicated; whether or not they are certainly and effectually applied and communicated to all for whom they were procured or purchased? We do not at present meddle with this question, in so far as it is affected by the materials we have for deciding it, in what we have the means of knowing, concerning the will, the decrees, the design, the purpose of the Father and the son in the matter, although this is manifestly an essential element in the decision; but only in so far as it is connected with certain views regarding the nature and the immediate objects and effects of Christ's sufferings and death; in other words, regarding the nature and import of the impetration or purchase of the blessings of reconciliation and pardon as set before us in Scripture. And here again, of course, our leading position is, as before, that such a view of the impetration of pardon and reconciliation, as does not also include or imply in it a certain and effectual provision for applying or communicating them to all for whom they were procured, does not come up to the full and fair import of the scriptural statements which unfold or indicate the immediate object and effect of the sufferings and death of Christ, and their bearing men's salvation, and upon all that salvation implies and requires,—especilly upon their pardon and reconciliation to God. An impetration which may possibly not be followed by application,—which, in many cases, will not be conjoined with the actual communication of what was procured,—which will leave many for whom it was undertaken and effected, to perish for ever, unpardoned and unreconciled,—does not correspond with, or come up to, the doctrines of substitution and satisfaction taught us in Scripture,—the information given us there concerning Christ's object in dying for men, and the bearing and consequences of His vicarious sufferings upon their relation to God, to His law, and to eternity.

Secondly, the second leading position implied in the defective and erroneous Arminian view, with respect to the immediate object and effect of Christ's death, is this,—that no causal or meritorious connection exists between it and faith and repentance, with which the application of, or actual participation in, the blessings of redemption, is inseparably connected. They teach that Christ procures pardon and reconciliation for all men upon condition of their repenting and believing; but they deny that, by dying, He procured for any man faith and repentance, or made any provision whatever for effecting or securing that any man should, in fact, repent or believe. The general principles of the Calvinistic scheme of doctrine, as distinguished from the Arminian, of course imply, that men cannot repent and believe of themselves, and that God in His good time, and in the execution of His own decrees and purposes, gives faith and repentance to all those, and to those only, whom He has chosen in Christ before the foundation of the world, and whom He has specially watched over, and attended to, in every step of the great process by which the salvation of sinners is ultimately accomplished; but here, again, in accordance with the plan and object we have repeatedly intimated, we advert at present only to the connection between the death of Christ and the production of faith and repentance in all in whom they are produced. Arminians differ among themselves as to the ability of men to repent and believe, and as to the kind and measure of divine agency that may be concerned in inducing or enabling men to repent and believe: the more consistent among them resolving the production of faith and repentance in each case into the powers or capacities of man himself; and the less consistent, but more evangelical, resolving it, with the sacred Scripture and the Calvinists, into the almighty agency of the Divine Spirit. But they all deny that Christ, by His sufferings and death, procured, or purchased, or merited faith and repentance for those who come at length to believe and repent. They all maintain that, whatever may be the cause or source of faith, it is not in any case one of the results of Christ's death,—one of the fruits of His purchase; it is not to be traced to the shedding of His precious blood, as if any causal connection existed between them,—as if the one exerted any meritorious or efficacious influence upon the other.

The reason of their unanimous maintenance of these views is very obvious. It Christ, by His sufferings and death, made provision for the production of faith, in order that thereby, in accordance with God's arrangements, men individually might actually partake in the blessings He procured for them,—it the production of faith is indeed one of the objects and results of His death, one of the fruits of His purchase,—then He could not have died for all men; He must have died only for those who ultimately believe; He must have made certain and effectual provision for applying and communicating redemption to all for whom He purchased it. And Calvinists undertake to show that Scripture sanctions the position, that faith, wherever it has been produced in any man, is to be traced to the death of Christ as its source or cause,—is to be regarded as one of the blessings purchased for him, and for all who are ever made partakers of it, by the shedding of Christ's blood, to prove this not only from particular statements of Scripture establishing this precise point, but also from the general representations given us there of the connection between the death of Christ, and not merely a general scheme of salvation for mankind at large, but the actual salvation of each man individually. The doctrine of our Confession upon the subject is this:* "The Lord Jesus, by His perfect obedience and sacrifice of Himself, which He through the eternal Spirit once offered up unto God, hath fully satisfied the justice of His Father; and purchased not only reconciliation, but an everlasting inheritance in the kingdom of heaven, for all those whom the Father hath given unto Him." Reconciliation was purchased by His sacrifice of Himself, and purchased for certain men. Along with this, and by the same price, was purchased for the same persons, an everlasting inheritance in the kingdom of heaven; and, of course, also that faith of theirs, with which both reconciliation and the everlasting inheritance are inseparably connected. The Arminians admit, that by His sacrifice He purchased for men reconciliation; but then they hold that, as it was purchased for all men, and as many men are never reconciled to God, what He purchased for any was not properly reconciliation, but rather what has been called reconcilability, or a capacity of being reconciled,—that is, the removing of legal obstacles, that they may all pass over, if they choose; the opening of a door, that they may all enter, if they are so disposed. And thus the substance of what they teach upon this point is this,—that, notwithstanding all that Christ did and suffered in order to save sinners, it was quite possible, so far as anything contemplated by, or involved in, the shedding of His blood was concerned,—so far as any provision was made by His humiliation and sacrifice for averting this result,—that no sinner might have been saved; that all for whom He died might perish for ever; that the everlasting inheritance in the kingdom of heaven might never have been enjoyed by any one of those whom He came to seek and to save, and for whose eternal happiness He poured our His blood.*

These are the leading peculiarities of the views commonly held by Arminian writers, in regard to this great doctrine of the atonement, though they are certainly not held with equal fulness and explicitness by all who may be fairly ranked under this general designation. Indeed, it will be found that the sounder Arminians, especially when they are engaged in defending the doctrine of the atonement against the Socinians, often bring out the doctrines of the substitution and satisfaction of Christ clearly and fully,—defend them with much learning and ability, and seem to understand them in a sense which, in consistency, ought to exclude all those views of theirs concerning the necessity of the atonement,—its nature,—its relation to the divine law,—and its immediate object and effect, which we have explained. But whenever they proceed to consider its bearing upon the condition and fate of men individually, in relation to God and eternity, and whenever they begin to unfold the doctrine of its universality, then we immediately discover the traces, more or less fully developed, of the errors and corruptions which I have stated and exposed.

My principal object in making this detailed statement of the peculiar views generally held by Arminians upon this subject, besides that of explaining one important department of the controversies that have been carried on regarding it, was to bring out these two considerations:

First, That Arminians have generally manifested a strong tendency to dilute or explain away the Scripture doctrines of the substitution and satisfaction of Christ; that, in their controversies with Calvinists upon this subject, they often greatly attenuate or modify the views which they themselves maintain, when defending the doctrine of the atonement against the Socinians; or at least refuse to follow them out to their legitimate consequences and applications, and thus obscure, and, to some extent, corrupt the great doctrine which most directly and immediately unfolds the foundation of a sinner's hope. Secondly, That this tendency of the Arminians to modify or explain away the Scripture doctrines of the substitution and satisfaction of Christ, and to approximate more or less to Socinian views, or at least to rest in vague and ambiguous generalities,—in loose and indefinite statements,—about the true nature, and the immediate objects and effects, of the sufferings and death of Christ, and the connection subsisting between them, is traceable to, or in some way intimately connected with, their doctrine of the universality of the atonement,—a consideration with strongly confirms the important position, that the nature of the atonement settles or determines its extent, and prepares us to expect to find, among all who hold a universal atonement,—Calvinists as well as Arminians,—the prevalence, in a greater or less degree, and with more or less or explicit development, of defective and erroneous views, with respect to the substitution and satisfaction of Christ, His bearing our sins in His own body, and by bearing them, bearing them way.

CHAPTER EIGHT

EXTENT OF THE ATONEMENT

We proceed not to the third and last division,—namely, the consideration of the peculiar views, in regard to the atonement, of those divines who profess to hold Calvinistic doctrines upon other points, but on this concur with, or approximate to, the views of the Arminians; and this, of course, leads us to examine the subject of the extent of the atonement,—a topic which is much discussed among theologians in the present day, and is, on this account, as well as from its own nature and bearings, possessed of much interest and importance.

There are now, and for more than two centuries,—that is, since the time of Cameron, a Scotsman, who became Professor of Theology in the Protestant Church of France,—there have always been, theologians, and some of them men of well-merited eminence, who have held the Calvinistic doctrines of the entire depravity of human nature, and of God's unconditional election of some men from eternity to everlasting life, but who have also maintained the universality of the atonement,—the doctrine that Christ died for all men, and not for those only who are ultimately saved. As some men have agreed with Arminians in holding the universality of the atonement who were Calvinists in all other respects, and as a considerable appearance of Scripture evidence can be produced for the doctrine that Christ died for all men, it has been generally supposed that the doctrine of particular redemption, as it is often called, or of a limited atonement, from the weak point of the Calvinistic system,—that which can with most plausibility be assailed, and can with most difficulty be defended. Now, this impression has some foundation. There is none of the Arminian doctrines, in favour of which so much appearance of Scripture evidence can be adduced, as that of the universality of the atonement; and if Arminians could really prove that Christ died for the salvation of all men, then the argument which, as I formerly intimated, they commonly deduce from this doctrine, in opposition to the Calvinistic doctrine of predestination, could not, taken by itself, be easily answered. It is evident, however, on the other side, that if the Arminian doctrine of the universality of the atonement can be disproved, when tried upon its own direct and proper grounds and evidences, without founding upon its apparent inconsistency with the other doctrines of the Calvinistic system, then not only is one important principle established, which has been held by most Calvinists,—that, namely, of a limited atonement, that is, of an atonement limited as to its destination or intended objects,—but great additional strength is given to the general body of the evidence in support of Calvinism.

This is the aspect in which the arrangement we have followed leads us to examine it. Looking merely at the advantage of controversial impression, it would not be the most expedient course to enter upon the Arminian controversy, as we are doing, through the discussion of the extent of the atonement, since Arminians can adduce a good deal that is plausible in support of its universality, and found a strong argument against Calvinistic predestination on the assumption of its universality,—considerations which would suggest the policy of first establishing some of the other doctrines of Calvinism against the Arminians, and then employing these doctrines, already established, to confirm the direct and proper evidence against a universal, and in favour of a limited, atonement. But since we have been led to consider the subject of an atonement in general, in opposition to the Socinians, we have thought it better to continue, without interruption, the investigation of this subject until we finish it, although it does carry us into the Arminian controversy, at the point where Arminianism seems to be strongest. We have though it better to do this than to return to the subject of the extent of the atonement, after discussing some of the other doctrines controverted between the Calvinists and the Arminians. And we have had the less hesitation about following out this order, for these reasons: first, because we are not afraid to encounter the Arminian doctrine of a universal atonement, upon the ground of its own direct and proper evidence, without calling in the assistance that might be derived from the previous proof of the other doctrines of Calvinism; secondly, because the examination of the whole subject of the atonement at once enables us to bring out more fully the principle, which we reckon of fundamental importance upon this whole question,—namely, that the nature of the atonement settles or determines its extent; and, thirdly, because, if it can be really shown, as we have no doubt it can, that the Scripture view of the nature, and immediate object and effect, of the atonement, disproves its universality, then we have, in this way, what is commonly reckoned the weakest part of the Calvinistic system conclusively established, on its own direct and proper evidence; and established, moreover, by the force of all the arguments which have been generally employed not only by Calvinists, but by the sounder or un-Socinianized Arminians, in disputing with the Socinians on the truth and reality of an atonement.

In proceeding now to advert to the subject of the extent of the atonement, as a distinct, independent topic, we shall first explain the doctrine which has been generally held upon this subject by Calvinists, commonly called the doctrine of particular redemption, or that of a limited or definite atonement; and then, secondly, advert to the differences between the doctrine of universal or unlimited atonement or redemption, as held by Arminians, and as held by those who profess Calvinistic doctrines upon other points.

The question as to the extent of the atonement, is commonly and popularly represented as amounting in substance to this: Whether Christ died for all men, or only for the elect,—for those who ultimately believe and are saved? But this state of the question does not bring out the true nature of the point in dispute with sufficient fulness, accuracy, and precision. And, accordingly, we find that neither in the canons of the Synod of Dort, nor in our Confession of Faith,—which are commonly reckoned the most important and authoritative expositions of Calvinism,—is there any formal or explicit deliverance given upon the question as stated in this way, and in these terms. Arminians, and other defenders of a universal atonement, are generally partial of this mode of stating it, because it seems most readily and obviously to give to their doctrine the sanction and protection of certain scriptural statements,—which look like a direct assertion,—but are not,—that Christ died for all men; and because there are some ambiguities about the meaning of the expressions, of which they usually avail themselves. I have no doubt that the controversy about the extent of the atonement is substantially decided in our Confession, through no formal deliverance is given upon the precise question, whether Christ died for all men, or only for the elect; and it may tend to bring out clearly the true state of the question, as well as contribute to the subsidiary, but still important, object of assisting to determine what is the doctrine of our Confession upon this subject, if we advert to the statements it contains regarding it, and the manner in which it gives its deliverance upon it. We have already had occasion to quote, incidentally, the principal declarations of the Confession upon this subject, in explaining the peculiar views of the Arminians, with regard to the atonement in general; but it may be proper now to examine them somewhat more fully. They are chiefly the following:* "They who are elected being fallen in Adam, are redeemed by Christ; are effectually called unto faith in Christ by His Spirit working in due season; are justified, adopted, sanctified, and kept by His power through faith unto salvation. Neither are any other redeemed by Christ, effectually called, justified, adopted, sanctified, and saved, but the elect only."

There are two questions which may be, and, indeed, have been, started with respect to the meaning of these words; attempts having been made to show that they do not contradict or exclude the doctrine of a universal atonement, as it has been sometimes held by Calvinists. The first question is as to the import of the word "redeemed;" and it turns upon this point,—Does the word describe merely the impetration or purchase of pardon and reconciliation for men by the death of Christ? or does it comprehend the application as well as the impetration? If it be understood in the first or more limited sense, as descriptive only of the impetration or purchase, then, of course, the statement of the Confession clearly asserts a definite or limited atonement,—comprehending as its objects those only who, in fact, receive all other spiritual blessing, and are ultimately saved; whereas, if it included the application as well as the impetration, the statement might consist with the universality of the atonement, as it is not contended, even by Arminians, that, in this wide sense, any are redeemed by Christ, except those who ultimately believe and are saved. Indeed, one of the principal uses to which the Arminians commonly apply the distinction between impetration and application, as they explain it, is this,—that they interpret the scriptural statements which seem to speak of all men as comprehended in the objects of Christ's death, of the impetration of pardon and reconciliation for them; and interpret those passages which seem to indicate some limitation in the objects of His dying, of the application of those blessings to men individually. Now, it seems very manifest that the word "redeemed" is to be taken here in the first, or more limited sense—as descriptive only of the impetration or purchase of pardon and reconciliation; because there is a distinct enumeration of all the leading steps in the great process which, originating in God's eternal, absolute election of some men, terminates in their complete salvation,—their redemption by Christ being evidently, from the whole structure of the statement, not comprehensive of, but distinguished from, their vocation and justification, which constitute the application of the blessing of redemption,—the benefits which Christ purchased.

The second question to which I referred, applies only to the last clause quoted,—namely, "neither are any other redeemed by Christ, effectually called, justified, adopted, sanctified, and saved, but the elect only." Here it has been made a question, whether the concluding restriction, to "the elect only," applies to each of the preceding predicates, "redeemed," "called," "justified," etc., singly and separately, or only to the whole of them taken collectively; that is, whether it be intended to be here asserted that not any one of these things, such as "redeemed," can be predicated of any but the elect only, or merely that the whole of them, taken in conjunction, cannot be predicated of any others. The latter interpretation,—namely, that there are none but the elect of whom the whole collectively can be predicated,—would make the declaration a mere truism, serving no purpose, and really giving no deliverance upon anything, although the repetition of the general statement about the consequences of election, or the execution of God's eternal decree, in a negative form, was manifestly intended to be peculiarly emphatic, and to contain a denial of an error reckoned important. The Confession, therefore, must be regarded as teaching, that it is not true of any but the elect only, that they are redeemed by Christ, any more than it is true that any others are called, justified, or saved. Here I may remark by the way, that though many modern defenders of a universal atonement regard the word redemption as including the application as well as the impetration of pardon and reconciliation,—and, in this sense, disclaim the doctrine of universal redemption,—yet a different phraseology was commonly used in theological discussions about the period at which the Confession was prepared, and in the seventeenth century generally. Then the defenders of a universal atonement generally maintained, without any hesitation, the doctrine of universal redemption,—using the word, of course, to describe only the impetration, and not the application, of spiritual and saving blessings; and this holds true, both of those who admitted, and of those who denied, the Calvinistic doctrine of election. Of the first of these cases (the Calvinists) we have an instance in Richard Baxter's work, which he entitled, "Universal Redemption of Mankind by the Lord Jesus Christ;" and of the second (the Arminians) in Dr Isaac Barrow's sermons, entitled, "The Doctrine of Universal Redemption Asserted and Explained."

The other leading statements upon this subject in the Confession, are those which we have already had occasion to quote from the eighth chapter, secs. 5, 8: "The Lord Jesus, by His perfect obedience and sacrifice of Himself, which He through the Eternal Spirit once offered up unto God, hath fully satisfied the justice of His Father; and purchased not only reconciliation, but an everlasting inheritance in the kingdom of heaven, for all those whom the Father hath given unto Him;" and again: "To all those for whom Christ hath purchased redemption" (that is, pardon and reconciliation), "He doth certainly and effectually apply and communicate the same; making intercession for them; and revealing into them, in and by the word, the mysteries of salvation; effectually persuading them by His Spirit to believe and obey," etc. Now, this latter statement, as I formerly intimated, contains, and was intended to contain, the true status question is in the controversy about the extent of the atonement. It is to be explained by a reference to the mode of conducting this controversy, between the Calvinists and Arminians, about the time of the Synod of Dort, and also to the mode of conducting the controversy excited in France by Cameron,* and afterwards carried on by Amyraldus in France and Holland, and by Baxter in England. The fundamental position of all who had advocated the doctrine of atonement against the Socinians, but had also maintained that it was universal or unlimited, was—that Christ, by His sufferings and death, purchased pardon and reconciliation for all men, without distinction or exception; but that these blessings are applied or communicated to, and, of course, are actually enjoyed by, those only who came, from whatever cause, to repent and believe. This, of course, is the only sense in which the doctrine of universal atonement, or redemption, could be held by any who did not believe in the doctrine of universal salvation. And the assertion or denial of this must, from the nature of the case, form the substance of the controversy about the extent of the atonement, whatever diversity of phrascology may be, at different times, employed in discussing it.

The doctrine of a universal atonement necessarily implies, not only that God desired and intended that all men should be benefited by Christ's death,—for this, in some sense, is universally admitted,—but that, in its special and peculiar character as an atonement,—that is, as a penal infliction, as a ransom price,—it should effect something bearing favourably upon their spiritual welfare. This could be only by its purchasing for all men the pardon of their sins and reconciliation with God, which the Scripture plainly represents as the proper and direct results or effects of Christ's death. The advocates of this doctrine accordingly say; that He impetrated or purchased these blessings for all men; and as many are never actually pardoned and reconciled, they are under the necessity, as I formerly explained, because they hold a universal atonement, both of explaining away pardon and reconciliation as meaning merely the removal of legal obstacles, or the opening up of a door, for God's bestowing these blessings, and of maintaining that these blessings are impetrated for many to whom they are never applied. Now this, of course, is the position which the statement in the Confession was intended to contradict, by asserting that impetration and application, though distinct, are co-extensive, and are never, in fact, separated,—that all for whom these blessings were ever designed or procured, do certainly receive them; or, conversely, that they were not designed, or procured, for any except those who ultimately partake of them. This, then, is the from in which the controversy about the extent of the atonement is stated and decided in our Confession of Faith; and, whatever differences of phraseology may have been introduced into the discussion of this subject in more modern times, it is always useful to ræur to this mode of stating the question, as fitted to explain the true nature of the points involved in it, and to suggest clear conceptions of the real import of the different topics adduced upon both sides. Those who are usually represented as holding the doctrine of particular redemption, or limited atonement,—as teaching that Christ did not die for all men, but only for the elect,—contend for nothing more than this, and cannot be shown to be under any obligation, in point of consistency, to contend for more,—namely, that, to all those for whom Christ hath purchased redemption, He doth certainly and effectually apply and communicate the same; and all who take the opposite side, and maintain that Christ died for all men,—that His atonement was universal or unlimited,—can, without difficulty, be proved to maintain, or to be bound in consistency to maintain,—if they really admit an atonement at all, and, at the same time, deny universal salvation,—that He purchased redemption—that is, pardon and reconciliation—for many to whom they are never applied, who never are put in possession of them.

We would now make two to three observations, suggested by this account of the state of the question. First, the advocates of a limited or definite atonement do not deny, but maintain, the infinite intrinsic sufficiency of Christ's satisfaction and merits. They regard His sufferings and death as possessed of value, or worth, sufficient to have purchased pardon and reconciliation for the whole race of fallen man. The value or worth of His sacrifice of Himself depends upon, and is measured by, the dignity of His person, and is therefore infinite. Though many fewer of the human race had been to be pardoned and saved, an atonement of infinite value would have been necessary, in order to procure for them these blessings; and though many more, yea, all men, had been to be pardoned and saved, the death of Christ, being an atonement of infinite value, would have been amply sufficient, as the ground or basis of their forgiveness or salvation. We know nothing of the amount or extent of Christ's sufferings in themselves. Scripture tells us only of their relation to the law, in compliance with the provision of which they were inflicted and endured. This implies their infinity, in respect of intrinsic legal worth or value; and this, again, implies their full intrinsic sufficiency for the redemption of all men, if God had intended to redeem and save them. There have been some Calvinists who have contended that Christ's sufferings were just as much, in amount or extent, as were sufficient for redeeming, or paying the ransom price of, the elect,—of those who are actually saved: so that, if more men had been to be pardoned and saved, Christ must have suffered more than He did, and if fewer, less. But those who have held this view have been very few in number, and of no great weight or influence. The opinion, however, is one which the advocates of universal atonement are fond of adducing and refuting, because it is easy to refute it; and because this is fitted to convey the impression that the advocates of a limited atonement in general hold this, or something like it, and thus to insinuate an unfavourable idea of the doctrine. There is no doubt that all the most emiuent Calvinistic divines hold the infinite worth or value of Christ's atonement,—its full sufficiency for expiating all the sins of all men.

A distinction was generally employed by the schoolmen, which has been often adverted to in this discussion, and which it may be proper to explain. They were accustomed to say, that Christ died sufficiently for all men, and efficaciously for the elect,—sufficienter pro omnibus, efficaciter pro electis. Some orthodox divines, who wrote before the extent of the atonement had been made the subject of full, formal, and elaborate discussion,—and Calvin himself among the rest,—admitted the truth of this scholastic position. But after controversy had thrown its full light upon the subject, orthodox divines generally refused to adopt this mode of stating the point, because it seemed to ascribe to Christ a purpose or intention of dying in the room of all, and of benefiting all by the proper effects of His death, as an atonement or propitiation; not that they doubted or denied the intrinsic sufficiency of His death for the redemption of all men, but because the statement—whether originally so intended or not—was so expressed as to suggest the idea, that Christ, in dying, desired and intended that all men should partake in the proper and peculiar effects of the shedding of His blood. Calvinists do not object to say that the death of Christ—viewed objectively, apart from His purpose or design—was sufficient for all, and efficacious for the elect, because this statement in the first clause merely asserts its infinite intrinsic sufficiency, which they admit; whereas the original scholastic form of the statement,—namely, that He died sufficiently for all,—seems to indicate that, when He died, He intended that all should derive some saving and permanent benefit from His death. The attempt made by some defenders of universal atonement to prove, that a denial of the universality of the atonement necessarily implies a denial of its universal intrinsic sufficiency, has nothing to do with the settlement of the state of the question, but only with the arguments by which the opposite side may be defended; and, therefore, I need not advert to it.

Secondly, It is not denied by the advocates of particular redemption, or of a limited atonement, that mankind in general, even those who ultimately perish, do derive some advantages or benefits from Christ's death; and no position they hold requires them to deny this. They believe that important benefits have accrued to the whole human race from the death of Christ, and that in these benefits those who are finally impenitent and unbelieving partake. What they deny is, that Christ intended to procure, or did procure, for all men those blessings which are the proper and peculiar fruits of His death, in its specific character as an atonement,—that He procured or purchased redemption—that is, pardon and reconciliation—for all men. Many blessings flow to mankind at large from the death of Christ, collaterally and incidentally, in consequence of the relation in which men, viewed collectively, stand to each other. All these benefits were, of course, foreseen by God, when He resolved to send His son into the world; they were contemplated or designed by Him, as what men should receive and enjoy. They are to be regarded and received as bestowed by Him, and as thus unfolding His glory, indicating His character, and actually accomplishing His purposes; and they are to be viewed as coming to men through the channel of Christ's mediation,—of His sufferings and death.*

The truth of this position has been considered as affording some warrant for saying, in a vague and indefinite sense, that Christ died for all men; and in this sense, and on this account, some Calvinists have scrupled about meeting the position that Christ died for all men with a direct negative, as if they might thus be understood as denying that there was any sense in which all men derived benefit, from Christ's death. But this position does not at all correspond with the proper import of what Scripture means when it tells us that Christ died for men. This, as we prove against the Socinians, implies that He substituted Himself in their room and stead, that He put Himself in their legal position, that He made satisfaction to God's justice for their sins, or that He purchased redemption for them; and this, we contend, does not hold true of any but those who are actually at length pardoned and saved. The advocates of universal atonement, then, have no right to change us with teaching that none derive any benefit from Christ's death except those who are pardoned and saved; we do not teach this, and we are not bound in consistency to teach it. We teach the opposite of this; and we are not deterred from doing so by the fear lest we should thereby afford to those who are opposed to us a medium for proving that, in the proper scriptural sense, He died for all men, or that the leading and peculiar benefits which His death procured for men,—the benefits of salvation,—were designed or intended for all mankind.

There is no very material difference between the state of the question with respect to the extent of the atonement,—and to that at present we confine our attention,—accordingly as its universality is maintained by Arminians, or by those who hold Calvinistic doctrines upon other points. The leading distinction is, that the Calvinistic universalists are obliged to practise more caution in their declarations upon some points, and to deal somewhat more in vague and ambiguous generalities than the Arminians, in order to avoid as much as possible the appearance of contradicting or renouncing, by what they say upon this subject, their professed Calvinism upon other topics.

As the controversy with regard to the extent of the atonement does not turn,—though many of the universalists would fain have it so,—upon the question of the infinite sufficiency of Christ's sufferings and merits, it must turn upon the question of the purpose, design, or intention of God in inflicting sufferings and death upon His Son, and of Christ in voluntarily submitting to them. Universal atonement thus indicates and proves the existence, on the part of God and Christ, of a purpose, design, or intention, in some sense or other, to save all men. And for the Calvinistic universalists to assert the existence of such a purpose, design, or intention,—in combination and in consistency with the doctrine that God has from eternity elected some men to everlasting life, and determined to save them,—requires the introduction of a good deal of confusion and ambiguity into their mode of stating and arguing the case. They cannot say, with the Arminians, that Christ died equally for all men; for they cannot dispute that God's special purpose of grace in regard to the elect,—which Arminians, deny, but they admit,—must have, in some sense and to some extent, regulated or influenced the whole of the process by which God's purpose was accomplished,—by which His decree of election was executed. They accordingly contend for a general design or purpose of God and Christ—indicated by the alleged universality of the atonement—to save all men; and a special design or purpose—indicated by the specialty of the bestowal of that faith (which they admit—which the Arminians, practically at least, deny—to be God's gift)—to save only the elect. But this, again, belongs rather to the argument of the case than to the state of the question. The substance of the matter is, that they concur with the Arminians in denying the great truth laid down in our Confession of Faith, that redemption,—that is, pardon and reconciliation,—are actually applied and communicated to all for whom they were procured or purchased; and, to a large extent, they employ the very same arguments in order to defend their position.

It may be worth while briefly to advert to one of the particular forms in which, in our own day, the state of the question has been exhibited by some of the Calvinistic universalists. It is that of asserting what they call a general and a special reference of Christ's death,—a general reference which it has to all men, and a special reference which it has to the elect. This is manifestly a very vague and ambiguous distinction, which may mean almost anything or nothing, and is, therefore, very well adapted to a transition state of things when men are passing from comparative ortho-doxy on this subject into deeper and more important error. This general reference of Christ's death,—its reference to all men,—may mean mere-ly, that, in consequence of Christ's death, certain benefits or advantages flow to mankind at large, and in this sense it is admitted by those who hold the doctrine of particular redemption; or it may describe the proper Arminian doctrine of universal or unlimited atonement; or, lastly, it may indicate anything or everything that may be supposed to lie between these two views. It cannot, therefore, be accepted as a true and fair account of the state of the question about the extent of the atonement, as discussed between Calvinists, and may not unreasonably be regarded with some jealousy and suspicion, as at least fitted, if not intended, to involve the true state of the question in darkness or ambiguity. The universality of the atonement had been defended before our Confession of Faith was prepared, by abler and more learned men,—both Calvinists and Arminians,—than any who in modern times have undertaken the same cause. The authors of the confession were thoroughly versant in these discussions; and it will be found, upon full study and investigation, that whatever variety of forms either the state of the question, or the arguments adduced on both sides, may have assumed in more modern discussion, the whole substance and merits of the case are involved in, and can be most fairly and fully discussed by, the examination of their position,—namely, that "to all those for whom Christ hath purchased redemption, He doth certainly and effectually apply and communicate the same. "This position proceeds upon the assumption that He purchased redemption for men. The truth of this assumption is involved in the establishment of the doctrine of the atonement,—of Christ's death being a ransom price,—in opposition to the Socinians, and must be admitted by all, unless, while professedly holding the doctrine of the atonement, they virtually sink down to Socinianism, by explaining it entirely away. And this being assumed, the position asserts, that all for whom redemption was purchased, have it applied or communicated to them; and that, of course, Christ died for the purpose, and with the intention, of procuring or purchasing pardon and reconciliation only for those who ultimately receive them, when they repent and believe.

CHAPTER NINE

EVIDENCE AS TO THE EXTENT OF THE ATONEMENT

I do not intend to enter here into anything like a full investigation of the scriptural evidence upon the subject of the extent of the atonement. I can only make a few observations upon some of the points involved in it,—suggesting some of the things that ought to be kept in view in the study of the subject; and in doing so, I need not hesitate, from any fear of being misunderstood, after the full explanations I have given about the true state of the question, to use, for the sake of brevity and convenience, the expressions, universal and limited atonement,—universal and particular redemption,—and Christ's dying for all men, or only for the elect.

The advocates of universal atonement confidently aver that this doctrine is clearly and explicitly taught in Scripture,—so clearly and explicitly, that it is to be taken as a first principle, and ought to regulate and control the interpretation and application of other passages which may seem inconsistent with it; and they appeal, in support of this position, to those scriptural statements which speak of Christ's dying or making propitiation for all,—for the world, the whole world,—and even, it is alleged, for some who do, or may, ultimately perish. We contend that these statements do not necessarily, or even naturally, bear the construction which our opponents put upon them; and that there are other scriptural statements which clearly indicate a limitation as to the persons whose spiritual welfare,—whose actual possession and enjoyment of any spiritual blessings,—was contemplated or intended by the death of Christ, or by Christ in dying. Our opponents, of course, profess to show that these statements may be all interpreted in accordance with their doctrine of the universality of the atonement. We profess to be able to assign good reasons why a language of a general, indefinite, or unlimited signification should have been employed in speaking of the objects and effects of Christ's death, while no full and proper universality was intended; and they profess to be able to assign good reasons why, in some cases, some limitation should be indicated, while yet there was no intention of denying that Christ died for all men,—that is, for all the individuals of the human race, pro omnibus et singulis. This is a general description of the way in which the controversy is conducted by the opposite parties, in the investigation of the scriptural evidence bearing more directly and immediately upon the subject of the extent of the atonement. It may be said to comprehend three leading departments: First, The investigation of the exact meaning and import of the principal passages adduced in support of the two opposite doctrines, especially with the view of ascertaining whether we can lay hold of any one position upon the subject which is distinct and definite, and does not admit, without great and unwarrantable straining, of being explained away, and which may therefore be regarded as a fixed point,—a regulating principle,—of interpretation. Secondly, The comparative facility and fairness with which the passages adduced on the opposite side may be explained, so as to be consistent with the position maintained; it being, of course, a strong argument in favour of the truth of any doctrine, that the passages adduced against it can be shown to be consistent with it, without its being necessary to have recourse to so much force and straining as are required in order to make the opposite doctrine appear to be consistent with the passages that are adduced against it. Thirdly, The investigation of the question, which doctrine is most consistent with a combined and harmonious interpretation of all the passages bearing upon the subject,—which of them most fully and readily suggests, or admits of, the laying down of general positions, that, when combined together, embrace and exhaust the whole of the information given us in Scripture regarding it.

Now, I believe that under each of these three heads it can be, and has been, shown, that the doctrine of a definite or limited atonement,—limited, that is, as to its destination and intended objects,—has a decided superiority over the opposite one, and is therefore to be received as the true doctrine of Scripture. It has a clearer and firmer support in particular statements of Scripture, that do not, plausibly or fairly, admit of being explained away. More obvious and satisfactory reasons can be assigned why indefinite and general language should be employed upon the subject, without its being intended to express absolute universality,—to include the whole human race, and all the individuals who compose it,—than can be adduced in explanation of language which indicates a limitation, if Christ died for all men. And, lastly, it is easier to present a combined and harmonious view of the whole information given us in Scripture upon the subject, if the doctrine of a limited or definite atonement be maintained, than if it be denied.

The materials of the first of these divisions consist exclusively of the examination of the meaning and import of particular text; and this is the basis and foundation of the whole argument. A very admirable and masterly summary of the direct scriptural evidence will be found in the first part of Dr candlish's recently published book on the atonement. I shall only make a few observations upon the topics comprehended in the other two heads.

No scriptural statements are, or even appear to be, inconsistent with the doctrine of a limited atonement, which merely assert or imply that Christ's sufferings were sufficient, in point of intrinsic worth and value, for the redemption of the whole human race; or that all men do, in fact, derive some benefits or advantages from Christ's death, and that God intended that they should enjoy these. We have already shown, in explaining the state of this question, that the advocates of a limited atonement do not deny, and are under no obligation in point of consistency to deny, these positions. Neither is it inconsistent with our doctrine, that God's sending, or giving, His Son should be represented as resulting from, and indicating, love to the world or to mankind in general,—φιλανθρωπια. If God intended that all men should derive some benefits and advantages from Christ's mediation, this may be regarded as indicating, in some sense, love or kindness to the human race in general, though He did not design or intend giving His Son to save every individual of the human family, or to do anything directed to that object. There is another race of fallen creatures under God's moral government, for whose salvation,—for the salvation of any of whom,—He made no provision. And God may be truly said to have loved the world, or the human race, or the family of man, as distinguished from, or to the exclusion of, the fallen angels; and as the result of this love, to have sent His Son, although He had no purpose of, and made no provision for, saving them all. On the other hand, it should be remembered, that Christ's dying for all men necessarily implies that God loved all men individually, and loved them so as to have, in some sense, desired and intended to save them; and that everything which proves that God did not desire and intend to save all men, equally proves that Christ did not die for them all; and that everything which must be taken in, to limit or modify the position that God desired and intended, or purposed, the salvation of all men, must equally limit or modify the position that Christ died for all. The scriptural evidence of these two positions is usually produced indiscriminately by the advocates of universal atonement, as equally proving their doctrine. And if, on the one hand, they afford each other some mutual countenance and support, so, on the other, they must be burdened with each other's difficulties, and must be both exposed to the explanations or modifications which each or either may suggest or require.

A favourite passage of our opponents is, "Who will have all men to he saved, and to come to the knowledge of the truth;" and again, "Who gave Himself a ransom for all."* Now, independently altogether of the clear evidence which the context furnishes—that the "all men" must mean men of all sorts, without any distinction of kinds or classes, and not all men, the whole human race, singly and individually,—it is plain that God will have all men to be saved, in the same sense, and with the same limitations and modifications, under which Christ gave Himself a ransom for all, and vice versa. And it is further evident, that God will have all men to be saved, in the same sense, and to the same extent only, in which "He will have all men to come to the knowledge of the truth." Now, we know that God does not, in any strict and proper sense, will all men (omnes et singulos) to come to the knowledge of the truth, though He has imposed upon all men who hear the truth an obligation to receive it; and it is proof sufficient that He does not will all men,—that is, understanding thereby all the individuals of the human, race,—to come to the knowledge of the truth, that there are, and have always been, very many of the human race from whom He has withheld the means and the opportunity of knowing it. And from all this taken together, it plainly follow, that these statements contain no warrant whatever for the doctrine, that God desired and intended the salvation of all the individuals of our race, or that Christ gave Himself a ransom for them all.

There is one great and manifest advantage which the doctrine of a limited atonement possesses over the opposite doctrine, viewed with reference to the comparative facility with which the language of Scripture can be interpreted, so as to accord with it; and this is, that it is much more easy to understand and explain how, in accordance with the ordinary sentiments and practice of men, general or indefinite language may have been employed, when strict and proper universality was not meant, than to explain why limited or definite language should ever have been employed, if there was really no limitation in the object or destination of the atonement. The fair principle of interpretation is, to make the definite and limited statements the standard for explaining the general and indefinite ones, and not the reverse; especially as Scripture furnishes many examples in which all the unlimited expressions that are applied to the death of Christ, viewed in relation to its objects,—the world, the whole world, all, every, etc.,—are used, when no proper and absolute, but merely a relative or comparative, universality was intended.

In addition, however, to this general consideration, which is evidently of great weight and importance, the defenders of a limited atonement assert, and undertake to prove, not only that there are scriptural statements which cannot, by any fair process of interpretation, be reconciled with the doctrine of universal atonement, but also, that in all the passages in which Christ is spoken of as dying for the world, or fur all, there is something in the passage or context which affords sufficient evidence that the all is not to be understood literally and absolutely as applicable to each and every individual of the human race, but with some restriction or limitation, according to the nature and relations of the subject treated of, or the particular object for which the statement is made. This position is thus expressed by Turretine in his chapter on the object of Christ's satisfaction:* "Nuspiam Christus dicitur in Scriptura pro omnibus mortuns, quin ibidem addatur limitatio, ex quâ colligitur hoc non universaliter, de omnibus et singulis esse intelligendum, sed restricte pro subjectâ materiâ." And though this position may, at first sight, seem a bold and startling one, I have no doubt it can be established by an examination of ALL the particular passages referred to; and I have always regarded the ease and certainty with which, in most cases, this limitation can be pointed out and proved, and the fair and reasonable evidence that can be adduced of it, in all cases as affording a very strong general corroboration of the truth of our doctrine. In many of these general and unlimited statements, the object is manifestly to indicate merely that those for whom Christ died are not confined to any one nation, class, or description of men,—the world, or the whole world, evidently meaning mankind at large, Gentiles as well as Jews,—a truth which it was then peculiarly necessary to enforce, and to bring out in the fullest and strongest terms, in consequence of the abuse made of the selection of the Jews as God's peculiar people. In not a few, a limitation is plainly indicated in the context as implied in the nature, relations, or characteristics of the of the general subject treated of; and, in several instances, a careful examination of passages which, when superficially considered and judged of merely by the sound, seem to favour the idea of a universal atonement, not only shows that they afford it no real countenance, but furnishes strong presumptions, if not positive proofs, against it. I am persuaded that most men who had not examined the subject with care, and had had pressed upon their attention the collection of texts usually adduced by the defenders of a universal atonement, would be somewhat surprised to find how quickly they evaporated before even a cursory investigation; and how very small was the residuum that really involved any serious difficulty, or required anything like straining to bring out of them a meaning that was perfectly consistent with the doctrine of particular redemption.

The case is widely different with the attempt of our opponents to harmonize with their views the passages on which our doctrine is more immediately founded. The more carefully they are examined, the more clearly will they be seen to carry ineradicable the idea of a limitation in the purpose or destination of the atonement, and of a firmly established and indissoluble connection between Christ's dying for men, and these men actually enjoying, in consequence, all spiritual blessings, and attaining ultimately to eternal salvation. And then, on the other hand, the attempts of our opponents to explain them, so as to make them consistent with the doctrine of universal atonement, are wholly unsuccessful. These attempts are commonly based, not on an examination of the particular passages themselves, or anything in their context and general scope, but upon mere indefinite and far-fetched considerations, which are not themselves sufficiently established to afford satisfactory solutions of other difficulties. Arminians commonly consider the passages which seem to indicate a limitation in the object of the atonement, as referring to the application, as distinguished and separated from the impetration or purchase of the blessings of redemption; while Calvinistic universalists usually regard them as referring to God's special design to secure the salvation of the elect, which they hold in combination with an alleged design or purpose to do something by means of a universal atonement, directed to the salvation of all men.

Now, independently of the consideration that these views of the two different classes of universalists are not themselves proved to be true, and cannot therefore be legitimately applied in this way, their application of them in this matter is liable to this fatal abjection, that in Scripture it is the very same things which are predicated of men, both with and without a limitation. The state of the case, is, not that the indications of limitation are exhibited when it is the application, and the indications of universality when it is the impetration, of spiritual blessings that is spoken of; nor, the one, when something peculiar to the elect, and other, when something common to mankind in general, is described. It is the same love of God to men, the same death of Christ, and the same ransom price paid for men, that are connected both with the limited and the unlimited phraseology. God loved the world, and Christ loved His church; Christ died for all, and He died for His sheep; He gave Himself a ransom for all, and He gave Himself a ransom for for many; and there is no warrant whatever for alleging that, in the one case, the love, and the death, and the ransom are descriptive of totally different things from what they describe in the other. The very same things are predicated of the two classes, the all and the sheep, the all and the many; and, therefore, the fair inference is, that they are not really two different classes, but one and the same class, somewhat differently described, and, of course, regarded under somewhat different aspects. The universalists, whether Arminians or Calvinists, do not predicate the same, but different things, of the two classes,—the all and the sleep, the all and the many,—while the Scripture predicates the same, and not different things, of both; and this consideration not only refutes the method of combining and harmonizing the various scriptural statements upon this subject adopted by our opponents, but shows the soundness and sufficiency of that which we propose. We say that Christ died, and gave His life a ransom for some men only,—those whom the Father had given Him; and not for all men,—that is, not for all the individuals of the human race, without exception,—but that those for whom He died are indeed all men, or mankind in general, without distinction of age or country, character or condition,—no class or description of men being excluded,—a sense in which we can prove that "all men" is often used in Scripture. And this combines in harmony the different statements which Scripture contains upon the subject: whereas the universalists are obliged, in order to harmonize scriptural statements, either to reject altogether the fair and natural meaning of those which represent Him as dying for some only, or also to maintain that He died for some men in one sense, and for all men, without exception, in a different sense; while they cannot produce, either from the particular passages, or from any other declarations of Scripture, evidence of the different senses in which they must understand the declarations, that He died for men, and gave Himself a ransom for them.*

CHAPTER TEN

EXTENT OF ATONEMENT AND GOSPEL OFFER

W ithout dwelling longer upon this topic of the mode of interpreting particular passages of Scripture, I would now advert briefly to some of the arguments for, and against, the doctrine of universal atonement, which are derived from more general considerations,—that is, from its consistency or inconsistency with other truths taught in Scripture, and with the general scheme of Scripture doctrine, or what is commonly called the analogy of faith.

By far the most important and plausible of the scriptural arguments in support of it, and the only one we mean to notice, is the alleged necessity of a universal atonement, or of Christ's having died for all men, as the only consistent ground or basis on which the offers and invitation of the gospel can be addressed indiscriminately to all men. We fully admit the

general fact upon which the argument is based,—namely, that in Scripture, men, without distinction and exception, have salvation, and all that
leads to it, offered or tendered to them,—that they are invited to come
to Christ and to receive pardon,—and assured that all who accept the
offer, and comply with the invitation, shall receive everything necessary
for their eternal welfare. We fully admit that God in the Bible does all
this, and authorizes and requires us to do the same in dealing with our
fellow-men. Very few Calvinists have ever disputed the propriety and the
obligation of addressing to men, indiscriminately, without distinction or
exception, the offers and invitations of Gospel mercy; and the few who
have fallen into error upon this subject,—such as Dr Gill, and some of
the ultra-Calvinistic English Baptists of last century,—have usually based
their refusal to offer to men indiscriminately pardon and acceptance,
and to invite any or all to come to Christ that they might receive these
blessings, upon the views they entertained, not about a limitation of the
atonement, but about the entire depravity of human nature,—men's
inability to repent and believe. This topic of the consistency of a limited
atonement with the unlimited offers and invitations of Gospel mercy, or
of the alleged necessity of a universal atonement as the only ground or
basis on which such offers and invitations can rest, has been very fully
discussed. We can only suggest a few hints in regard to it.

There are obviously two questions that may be entertained upon
this this subject: First, Is an unlimited atonement necessary in order
to warrant ministers of the gospel, or any who may be seeking to lead
others to the saving knowledge of the truth, to offer to men, without
exception, pardon and acceptance, and to invite them to come to Christ?
And, secondly, Is an unlimited atonement necessary in order to warrant
God in addressing, and in authorizing and requiring us to address, such
universal offers and invitations to our fellow-men? The neglect of keep-

ing these two questions distinct, has sometimes introduced error and confusion into the discussion of this subject. It is the first question with which we have more immediately to do, as it affects a duty which we are called upon to discharge; while the second is evidently, from its very nature, one of those secret things which belong unto the Lord. It is very evident that our conduct, in preaching the gospel, and in addressing our fellow-men with a view to their salvation, should not be regulated by any inferences of our own about the nature, extent, and sufficiency of the provision actually made for saving them, but solely by the directions and instructions which God has given us, by precept or example, to guide us in the matter,—unless, indeed, we venture to act upon the principle of refusing to obey God's commands, until we fully understand all the grounds and reasons of them. God has commanded the gospel to be preached to every creature; He has required us to proclaim to our fellow-men, of whatever character, and in all varieties of circumstances, the glad tidings of great joy,—to hold out to them, in His name, pardon and acceptance through the blood of atonement,—to invite them to come to Christ, and to receive Him,—and to accompany all this with the assurance that "whosoever cometh to Him, He will in no wise cast out." God's revealed will is the only rule, and ought to be held to be the sufficient warrant for all that we do in this matter,—in deciding what is our duty,—in making known to our fellow-men what are their privileges and obligations,—and in setting before them reasons and motives for improving the one and discharging the other. And though this revelation does not warrant us in telling them that Christ died for all and each of the human race,—a mode of preaching the gospel never adopted by our Lord and His apostles,—yet it does authorize and enable us to lay before men views and considerations, facts and argument, which, in right reason, should warrant and persuade all to whom they are addressed, to lay hold of the hope set before them,—to turn into the stronghold as prisoners of hope.

The second question, as to the conduct of God in this matter, leads into much greater difficulties,—but difficulties which we are not bound, as we have no ground to expect to be able, to solve. The position of our opponents is, in substance, this,—that it was not possible for God, because not consistent with integrity and uprightness, to address such offers and invitations to men indiscriminately, unless an atonement, which is indispensable to salvation, had been presented and accepted on behalf of all men,—of each individual of the human race. Now, this position bears very manifestly the character of unwarranted presumption, and assumes our capacity of fully comprehending and estimating the eternal purposes of the divine mind,—the inmost grounds and reasons of the divine procedure. It cannot be proved,—because there is really not any clear and certain medium of probation,—that God, by offering to men indiscriminately, without distinction or exception, through Christ, pardon and acceptance, contradicts the doctrine which He has revealed to us in His own word, as to a limitation, not in the intrinsic sufficiency, but in the intended destination of the atonement. And unless this can be clearly and conclusively proved, we are bound to believe that they are consistent with each other, though we may not be able to perceive and develop this consistency, and, of course, to reject the argument of our opponents as untenable. When we carefully analyze all that is really implied in what God says and does, or authorizes and requires us to say and do in this matter, we can find much that is fitted to show positively that God does not, in offering pardon and acceptance to men indiscriminately, act inconsistently or deceptively, though it is not true that the atonement was universal. And it is easy to prove that He does no injustice to any one; since all who believe what He has revealed to them, and who do what he has given them sufficient motives or reasons for doing, will certainly obtain salvation. And although difficulties will still remain in the matter, which cannot be fully solved, it is easy to show that they just resolve into the one grand difficulty of all religion and of every system of theology,—that, namely, of reconciling, or rather of developing, the consistency between the supremacy and sovereignty of God, and the free agency and responsibility of man. In arguing with Calvinistic universalists, there is no great difficulty in showing that the principles on which they defend their Calvinistic views, upon other points, against Arminian objections, are equally available for defending the doctrine of a limited atonement against the objection we are considering; and that the distinction which they attempt to establish between the two cases are either altogether unfounded, or, if they have some truth and reality in them (as, for instance, that founded on the difference between natural and moral inability,—a distinction which seems to have been first fully developed by Cameron, and with a special view to this very point), do not go to the root of the matter,—do not affect the substance of the case,—and leave the grand difficulty, though slightly altered in the position it occupies, and in the particular aspect in which it is presented, a strong and formidable as ever.

Though the advocates of a universal atonement are accustomed to boast much of the support which, they allege, their doctrine derives from the scriptural statements about God's loving the world,—Christ's dying for all; yet many of them are pretty well aware that they really have but little that is formidable to advance, except the alleged inconsistency of the doctrine of a limited atonement with the unlimited or indiscriminate offers of pardon and acceptance,—the unlimited or indiscriminate invitations and commands to come to Christ and to lay hold on Him,—which God address to men in His word, and which He has authorized and required us to address to our fellow-men. The distinction between the ground and warrant of men's act, and of God's act, in this matter, not only suggests materials for answering the arguments of opponents, but it also tends to remove a certain measure of confusion, or misconception, sometimes exhibited upon this point by the defenders of the truth. Some of them are accustomed to say, that the ground or warrant for the universal or unlimited offers of pardon, and commands to believe, is the infinite intrinsic sufficiency of Christ's atonement, which they generally hold, though denying its universal intended destination or efficiency; while others profess to rest the universal offers and commands upon the simple authority of God in His word,—making them Himself, and requiring us to proclaim them to others.

Now, it is evident that these two things are not, as the language of some orthodox divines might lead us to suppose, contrasted with, or opposed to, each other. The sole ground or warrant for men's act, in offering pardon and salvation to their fellow-men, is the authority and command of God in His word. We have no other warrant than this; we need no other; and we should seek or desire none; but on this ground alone should consider ourselves not only warranted, but bound, to proclaim to our fellow-men, whatever be their country, character, or condition, the good news of the kingdom, and to call upon them to come to Christ that they may be saved,—the Bible affording us sufficient, yea, abundant materials for convincing them that, in right reason, they ought to do this, and for assuring them that all who do, shall obtain eternal life. But this has manifestly nothing to do with the question, as to the ground or warrant of God's act in making unlimited offers, and in authorizing us to make them.

In regard to the allegation often made by orthodox divines, that this act of God is warranted by, and is based upon, the infinite intrinsic sufficiency of Christ's atonement, we would only remark,—for we cannot enter into the discussion,—that we are not aware of any Scripture evidence that these two things,—namely, the universal intrinsic sufficiency and the unlimited offers,—are connected in this way,—that we have never been able to see how the assertion of this connection removed or solved the difficulty, or threw any additional light upon this subject,—and that, therefore, we think it best while unhesitatingly doing ourselves, in our intercourse with our fellow-men, all that God's word authorizes and requires, to be contented with believing the general position,—that God in this, as in everything else, has chosen the best and wisest means of accomplishing all that He really intended to effect; and to be satisfied,—so far as the objection of opponents is concerned,—with showing, that it cannot be proved that there is any inconsistency or insincerity, that there is any injustice or deception, on God's part, in anything which He says or does in this matter, even though the intended destination of the atonement was to effect and secure the forgiveness and salvation of the elect only,—even though He did not design or purpose, by sending His Son into the world, to save any but those who are saved.

CHAPTER ELEVEN

EXTENT OF ATONEMENT, AND ITS OBJECT

W e must now notice the arguments against the doctrine of universal atonement derived from doctrines or principles taught in Scripture, as distinguished from particular scriptural statements bearing immediately upon the precise point; leaving out of view, however, in the meantime, and in the first instance, for reasons formerly stated, the arguments derived from its inconsistency with the doctrine of election, or any of what are commonly reckoned the peculiarities of Calvinism. The leading scriptural arguments against the doctrine of universal atonement, in the sense and with the limitation just explained, are these: First, that it is inconsistent with the scriptural account of the proper natural, and immediate objects and effects, of the sufferings and death of Christ, as a vicarious atonement; and, secondly, that it is in consistent with the scriptural account of the invariable and certain connection between the impetration or purchase, and the application to men individually, of all spiritual blessings. The second general argument admits of being broken down into several different divisions, or distinct positions, each of which can be established by its own appropriate scriptural evidence,—as, first, that "the oblation or sacrifice and intercession of Christ are one entire means respecting the accomplishment of the same proposed end, and have the same personal object,"—a proposition elaborately established by Dr Owen, whose words I have adopted in stating it:* and secondly, that the operation of the Holy Spirit, in producing faith and regeneration in men individually, and faith and regeneration themselves viewed as the gifts of God, are the fruits of Christ's satisfaction and obedience, and are conferred upon all in whose room He suffered and died. If these doctrines be true, they manifestly preclude the idea of an atonement that was universal, unlimited, or indefinite in its destination or intended objects and effects. But I will not dwell upon any of this class of topics, though they are very important,—and will only make some observations upon the inconsistency of the doctrine of an unlimited atonement, with scriptural views of the proper nature and immediate objects and effects of Christ's death, in further illustration of the important principle, which has been repeatedly adverted to,—namely, that the nature of the atonement settles or determines the question of its extent.

The plan usually adopted by the universalists in discussing this fundamental department of the subject, is to lay down an arbitrary definition of what atonement means in general, or in the abstract, and this definition of theirs usually amounts, in substance, to something of this sort,—namely, that an atonement is an expedient, or provision,—any expedient or provision,—whereby the great ends of law and government may be promoted and secured, without its being necessary to inflict the penalty of the law upon those who had incurred it by transgression; thus removing obstacles and opening a door to their being pardoned.

If this definition really embraced all that the Scripture makes known to us concerning the nature and immediate objects of the atonement of Christ, then it might possibly be universal or unlimited; for, according to this view, it was fitted and intended only to make the pardon and salvation of sinners possible,—to leave it free and open to God to pardon any or all of them, as He might choose.

Now, we do not say that this definition of an atonement, as applied to the death of Christ, is false; though some of the terms in which it is usually embodied—such as an expedient—are not very suitable or becoming. It is, in substance, a true description of the death of Christ, so far as it goes,—just as the Socinian view of it, as a testimony and an example, is true. The definition to which we have referred is really suggested by some scriptural views of what the death of Christ was, and of what it was intended to effect. And it accords also with some of the analogies suggested by human government and laws. What we maintain upon this point is, that it does not present a full and complete definition or description of the nature and immediate objects of the death of Christ, as they are represented to us in Scripture; and that therefore it is altogether unwarrantable to lay it down as the definition of an atonement, by which we are to judge—for this is practically the application the universalists make of their definition—of what an atonement must be, and of what views we ought to take of Christ's death. The analogies suggested by the principles of human government, and the applications of human laws,—though they are not without their use in illustrating this matter,—must be very imperfect. The death of One, who was at once a possessor of the divine nature, and at the same time a perfectly holy and innocent man, and whose death was intended to effect the salvation of men who, by transgression, had become subject to the wrath and curse of God, must necessarily be altogether unique and sui generis, and must not be estimated or judged of by any antecedent conception, or comprehended in any arbitrary definitions of ours. We can comprehend it only by taking in the whole of the information which Scripture communicates to us regarding it; we can define and describe it aright only by embodying all the elements which have scriptural warrant or sanction. An atonement is just that, be it what it may, which the death of Christ was; and the proper definition of an atonement is that which takes in all, and not only some, of the aspects in which the death of Christ is actually presented to us in Scripture. That it was a great provision for securing the ends of government and law, even while transgressors were pardoned and saved,—that it embodies and exhibits most impressive views of the perfections of God, of the excellence of His law, and of the sinfulness of sin,—that it affords grounds and reasons on which transgressors may be pardoned and saved, while yet the great principles of God's moral government are maintained, and its ends are secured;—all this is true important, but all this does not exhaust the scriptural views of the death of Christ, and therefore it should not be set forth as constituting the definition of an atonement. The Scripture tells us something more than all this, by giving more definite and specific information concerning the true nature of Christ's death, and the way and manner in which, from its very nature, it is fitted to effect, and does effect, its immediate intended objects. These considerations may be of some use in leading us to be on our guard against the policy usually pursued by the universalists, in paying the way for the introduction of their views, and providing for themselves a shield against objections, by laying down an arbitrary and defective definition of an atonement.

The two leading ideas, which are admitted to be involved in the doctrine of the atonement by almost all who repudiate Socinian views, are—as we formerly explained at length—substitution and satisfaction.

And the substance of what we maintain upon the subject now under consideration is just this,—that these two ideas, when understood in the sense in which Scripture warrants and requires us to understand them, and when clearly and distinctly realized, instead of being diluted and explained away, preclude and disprove the doctrine of a universal atonement. Substitution—or taking the place and acting in the room and stead of others—naturally and obviously suggests the notion, that these others, whose place was taken—in whose room or stead something was done or suffered—were a distinct and definite class of persons, who were conceived of, and contemplated individually, and not a mere indefinite mass indiscriminately considered. Mediation, or interposition in behalf of others, understood in a general and indefinite sense, without any specification of the nature or kind of the mediation or interposition, may respect a mass of men, viewed indiscriminately and in the gross; but mediation or interposition, in the form or by means of substitution in their room, or taking their place, naturally suggests the idea that certain particular men were contemplated, whose condition and circumstances individually were known, and whose benefit individually was aimed at. This idea is thus expressed by Witsius:* "Neque fieri nobis ullo modo posse videtur, ut quis Christum pro omnibus et singulis hominibus mortnum ex animi sententia cotendat, nisi prius enervata phrasi illa pro aliquo mori, quâ substitutionem in locum alterins notari nuper contra Socinianos evicimus." Witsius thought that no man could honestly and intelligently contend for the truth of the doctrine, that Christ had died for all men, until he had first enervated or explained away what was implied in the phrase, of dying in the room and stead of another; and there is much in the history of theological discussion to confirm this opinion.

This extract, however, from Witsius, reminds us that the doctrine of the atonement, as maintained against the Socinians, includes the idea, not only of substitution, but also of satisfaction; and the examination of this notion affords clearer and more explicit evidence that Christ did not die for all men, or for any who ultimately perish. If anything be really established in opposition to the Socinians upon this subject, it is this,—that Christ not only took the place, or substituted Himself in the room and stead of sinners, but that He suffered and died in their room and stead,—that is, that He suffered what was due to them, and what, but for His sufferings it in their stead, they must have endured. Of course we do not found upon the idea,—for, as we have already explained, we do not believe it to be true,—that Christ's sufferings, in point of amount and extent, were just adequate to satisfy for the sins of a certain number of persons. We have no doubt that He would have endured no more, though many more had been to be saved. Still, His sufferings were the endurance of a penal infliction. And they were the endurance of the penalty which me had incurred,—of that penalty itself, or of a full equivalent for it, in point of legal worth or value, and not of a mere substitute for it, as the universalists commonly allege. The law, which men had broken, appointed a penalty to each of them individually,—a penalty to the infliction of which each was individually liable. And unless the law was to be wholly relaxed or set aside, there must, for each individual who had transgressed, be the compliance with the law's demands,—that is, the infliction of this penalty, either upon himself, or on a substitute acting—qualified to act—and accepted as acting, in his room and stead. The transgression was personal, and so must be the infliction of the penalty. If the transgression, and the corresponding infliction of the penalty, were in their nature personal, and had respect to men individually, so, in like manner, must any transactions or arrangements that might be contemplated and adopted with a view to the transference of the penalty: so that, it being borne by another, those in whose room He bore it might escape unpunished, the law being satisfied by another suffering the penalty which it prescribed in their stead.

The Scripture, however, not only represents Christ, in suffering and dying, as substituting Himself in our room,—as enduring the penalty which we had incurred, and must otherwise have endured,—and as thus satisfying the divine justice and law in our stead; but also as thereby reconciling men to God, or purchasing for then reconciliation and pardon. This, the direct and immediate effect of the death of Christ, in its bearing upon men's condition, naturally and necessarily suggests the idea of a distinct and definite number of persons in whose behalf it was effected, and who are at length certainly to receive it. It is not reconcilability, but reconciliation, that the Scripture represents as the immediate object or effect of Christ's death: and this implies a personal change in the relation of men individually to God. And it is no sufficient reason for explaining this away, as meaning something far short of the natural and obvious import of the words, that men individually were not reconciled when Christ died, but receive reconciliation and pardon individually during their abode upon earth, according as God is pleased effectually to call them. We assume,—as we are fully warranted in doing,—that reconciliation with God and forgiveness of sin, where ever they are possessed and enjoyed, in any age or country, stand in the same relation to the death of Christ, as the reconciliation and pardon which the apostles enjoyed, are represented by them as doing; and that is, that they were immediately procured or purchased by it, and that their application, in due time, to all for whom they were purchased, was effectually secured by it. If this be the relation subsisting between the death of Christ and the reconciliation and pardon of sinners, He must, in dying, have contemplated, and provided for, the actual reconciliation and pardon of men individually,—that is, of all those, and of those only, who ultimately receive these blessings, whatever other steps or processes may intervene before they are actually put in possession of them.

The leading peculiar view generally held by Arminians,—at least those of them who bring out their views most fully and plainly,—are, as we formerly explained, these: first, that they do not regard Christ as suffering the penalty due to sinners, nor even a full equivalent—an adequate compensation—for it, but only a substitute for it; secondly, that there was a relaxation of the law in the forgiveness of sinners, not merely in regard to the person suffering, but also the penalty suffered, since it was not even in substance executed; and, thirdly, that the direct immediate effect of Christ's death was not to procure for men reconciliation and pardon, but merely to remove legal obstacles, and to open a door for God bestowing these blessings on any men, or all men. These views they seem to have been led to adopt by their doctrine about the universality of an atonement; and as the universality of the atonement naturally leads to those methods of explaining, or rather explaining away, its nature,—its relation to the law, and its immediate object and effect,—the establishment and application of the true scriptural views of substitution, satisfaction, and reconciliation, as opposed to the three Arminian doctrines upon these points stated above, exclude or disprove its universality,—or its intended destination to any but those who are ultimately pardoned and saved. Substitution, satisfaction, and reconciliation may be so explained,—that is, may be wrapped up in such vague and ambiguous generalities,—as to suggest no direct reference to particular men, considered individually, as the objects contemplated and provided for in the process; but the statements of Scripture, when we carefully investigate their meaning, and realize the ideas which they convey,—and which they must convey, unless we are to sink down to Socinianism,—bring these topics before us in aspects which clearly imply that Christ substituted Himself in the room of some men, and not of all men,—that all for whose sins He made satisfaction to the divine justice and law, certainly receive reconciliation and pardon,—and that, when they do receive them, they are bestowed upon each of them on this ground that Christ suffered in his room and stead, expiated his sins upon the cross, and thereby effectually secured his eternal salvation, and everything that this involves.

It has been very ably and ingeniously argued, in opposition to the doctrine of universal atonement, and especially in favour of the consistency of the unlimited offers of the gospel with a limited atonement, that the thing that is offered to men in the gospel is just that which they actually receive, and become possessed of, when they individually accept the offer; and that this is nothing vague and indefinite,—not a mere possibility and capacity,—but real, actual reconciliation and pardon. This is true, and very important; but the process of thought on which the argument is based, might be carried further back, even into the very heart and essential nature of the atonement, in this way. What men receive when they are individually united to Christ by faith,—that is, actual reconciliation and pardon,—is that which is offered or tendered to them before they believe. But that which is offered to them before they believe, is just that which Christ impetrated or purchased for them; and what it was that Christ impetrated or purchased for them depends upon what was the true nature and character of His death. And if His death was indeed a real satisfaction to the divine justice and law in men's room, by being the endurance in their stead of the penalty due to them,—and in this way affording ground or reason for treating them as if they had never broken the law, or as if they had fully borne in their own persons the penalty which it prescribed,—we can thus trace through the whole process by which sinners are admitted into the enjoyment of God's favour, a necessary reference to particular men considered individually, a firm and certain provision for the reconciliation and pardon of all for whom, or in whose stead, Christ died, for purchasing redemption only for those who were to be ultimately saved, and, of course, for applying its blessings to all for whom they were designed.

Those more strict and definite views of substitution, satisfaction, and reconciliation, which thus exclude and disprove an unlimited or indefinite atonement, that did not respect particular men, viewed individually, while clearly sanctioned by scriptural statements, can also be shown to be necessarily involved in the full and consistent development, even of those more defective views which the universalists would substitute in their room. The death of Christ, according to them, operates upon men's relation to God and their external welfare, not by its being an endurance of the penalty of the law in their room, and thus satisfying divine justice, but merely by its being suffering inflicted vice pœnœ, as we saw in Limborch, or as a substitute for the penalty; and as thus presenting certain views of God's character, government, and law, which, when impressed upon men's minds, would prevent any erroneous view, or any injurious consequences, arising from their sins being pardoned. Now,—not to dwell again upon the serious objection to this principle, when set forth as a full account of the doctrine of the atonement, from its involving no provision whatever for the actual exercise, but only for the apparent outward manifestation, of the divine perfections,—it is important to notice, that it is not easy to see how the death of Christ is fitted to produce the requisite impressions, unless it be really regarded in the light in which Scripture represents it, as the endurance, of the penalty of the law in our room and stead. In order to serve the purposes ascribed to it, as an expedient of government, by producing certain impressions upon men's minds, it must unfold the holiness and justice of God,—the perfection and unchangeableness of His law,—and the exceeding sinfulness and infinite danger of sin. Now, it is not merely true, as we contend, in opposition to the Socinians, that these impressions can be produced, and the corresponding results can be accomplished, only by an atonement,—only by substitution and satisfaction, understood in some vague and indefinite sense,—but also that, in order to this, there must be true substitution, and real and proper satisfaction. The justice and holiness of God are very imperfectly, if at all, manifested, by His inflicting some suffering upon a holy and innocent person, in order that sinners might escape, unless that person were acting, and had consented to act, strictly as the surety and substitute of those who were to receive the benefit of His sufferings.

There is certainly no manifestation of the excellence and perfection of the divine law, or of the necessity of maintaining and honouring it, if in the provision made for pardoning sinners, it was relaxed and set aside,—if its penalty was not inflicted,—if there was no fulfilment of its exactions, no compliance with its demands. It is only when we regard the death of Christ in its true scriptural character, and include, in our conceptions of it, those more strict and definite views of substitution and satisfaction, which exclude the doctrine of universal atonement, that we can see, in the pardon of sinners, and in the provision made for effecting it, the whole combined glory of God's moral character, as it is presented to us in the general statements of Scripture, and that we can be deeply impressed with right conceptions of the perfection of the divine law, and of the honour and reverence that are unchangeably due to it. The notion, then, that the atonement operates upon the forgiveness of sinners, merely by its being a great display of the principles of God's moral government,—and this is the favourite idea in the present day of those who advocate a universal atonement,—is not only liable to the fatal objection of its giving defective, and, to some extent, positively erroneous views of the nature of the atonement, as it is represented to us in Scripture, but is, moreover, so far from being fitted to be a substitute for, and to supersede the stricter views of, substitution and satisfaction, that it cannot stand by itself,—that nothing can really be made of it, unless those very views which it was designed to supersede are assumed as the ground or basis on which it rests.

I had occasion to mention before, that there was a considerable difference in the degree to which the Arminians allowed their doctrine of the extent of the atonement to affect their representations and dilutions of its nature and immediate object, and that they usually manifested more soundness upon this subject when contending against the Socinians, than when attacking the Calvinists. It has also generally held true, that Calvinistic universalists have not gone quite so far in explaining away the true nature of the atonement as the Arminians have done. They have, however, generally given sufficiently plain indications of the perverting and injurious influence of the doctrine of universal atonement upon right views of its nature, and never perhaps so fully as in the present day. There are men in the present day, who still profess to hold Calvinistic doctrines upon some points, who have scarcely left anything in the doctrine of the atonement which a Socinian would think it worth his while to oppose. I do not now refer to those who are popularly known amongst us by the name of Morisonians; for though they began with merely asserting the universality of the atonement, they made very rapid progress in their descent from orthodoxy; and through of but a very few years' standing under this designation, they have long since renounced everything Calvinistic, and may be justly regarded as now teaching a system of gross, unmitigated Pelagianism. There are others, however,

both in this country and in the United States, who, while still professing
to hold some Calvinistic doctrines, have carried out so fully and so far
their notion of the atonement being not a proper substitution or satisfaction, but a mere display, adapted to serve the purpose of God's moral
government, that it would really make no very essential difference in
their general scheme of theology, if they were to renounce altogether the
divinity of our Saviour, and to represent His death merely as a testimony
and an example.

Perhaps it is but just and fair to be somewhat more explicit and personal upon this point, and to say plainly whom, among the defenders
of a universal atonement in our own day, I mean,—and whom I do not
mean,—to comprehend in this description. I mean to comprehend in it
such writers as Dr Beman in America, and Dr Jenkyn in this country;
and I do not mean to comprehend in it Dr Wardlaw and Dr Payne,
and writers who agree in defending, in their way, the doctrine of a
universal atonement. Dr Beman and Dr Jenkyn both teach, that the
death of Christ was a mere substitute for the penalty which the law had
prescribed, and which men had incurred; and that it operates upon the
forgiveness of men's sins, not by its being a proper satisfaction to the
divine justice and law, but merely by its being a display of principles, the
impression of which upon men's minds is fitted to promote and secure
the great ends of God's moral government, while they are receiving the
forgiveness of their sins, and are admitted into the enjoyment of God's
favour. Dr Wardlaw, on the contrary, has always asserted the substance
of the scriptural doctrine of the atonement, as involving the ideas of
substitution and satisfaction; and has thus preserved and maintained
one important and fundamental branch of scriptural truth, in the defence of which, indeed, against the Socinians, he has rendered important
services to the cause of scriptural doctrine. The injurious tendency of

the doctrine of universal or unlimited atonement upon his views of its
nature (for it will be recollected, that I at present leave out of view the
connection between this doctrine and the peculiarities of the Calvinistic
system), appear chiefly in these respects: first, the exaggerated importance which he sometimes attributes to the more manifestation of the
general principles of the divine moral government, as distinguished from
the actual exercise of the divine perfections, and the actual fulfilment
and enforcement of the divine law, in the great process adopted for
pardoning and saving sinners; and, secondly, in occasional indications of
dissatisfaction with some of the more strict and definite views of substitution and satisfaction, without any very distinct specification of what it
is in these views to which he objects.* It is not, indeed, to be supposed,
that these statements bring out the whole of the perverting influence of
the doctrine of universal atonement upon Dr Wardlaw's views on this
subject, for, while this is the whole extent to which he has developed
its effects upon his views of the proper nature and immediate effect of
the atonement, he of course supports the important error (as every one
who holds and unlimited atonement must do), that Christ, by dying,
did not purchase or merit faith and regeneration for His people; and
that, consequently, so far as depended upon anything that the atonement
effected or secured, all men might have perished, even though Christ died
to save them. But it must be recollected, that this department, too, of the
subject I set aside, as one on the discussion of which I should not enter,
confining myself to some illustration of the inconsistency of the doctrine
of universal atonement, with right views of the nature and immediate
effect of the atonement, and of its powerful tendency to lead men who,
in the main, hold scriptural views upon these subjects, to dilute them or
explain them away.

It is very common for men who hold loose and erroneous views in regard to substitution and satisfaction, to represent the stricter and more definite views of these subjects, which are necessarily connected with the doctrine of a limited atonement, as leading to Antinomianism. But there is no great difficulty in defending them against this objection; for it is easy enough to show that the highest and strictest views upon these points, which have received the sanction of Calvinists, do not afford any ground for the general position that the law is abrogated or set aside, even in regard to believers,—and are perfectly consistent with the truth that they are still subject to its obligation, as a rule of life, though they are not under it "as a covenant of works, to be thereby justified or condemned;"* while it can also be easily shown that they afford no countenance to the notions of some men—who approximate to Antinomianism—about the eternal justification of the elect, or their justification, at least, from the time when the sacrifice of Christ in their room was first accepted,—notions sufficiently refuted by these general positions; first, that the substitution and satisfaction of Christ form part of a great and consistent scheme, all the parts of which are fitted to, and indissolubly linked with, each other; and, secondly, that it is one of the provisions of this great scheme, that, to adopt the language of our Confession† though "God did, from all eternity, decree to justify all the elect; and Christ did, in the fulness of time, die for their sins, and rise again for their justification; nevertheless they are not justified, until the Holy Spirit doth in due time actually apply Christ unto them."

CHAPTER TWELVE

EXTENT OF ATONEMENT, AND CALVINISTIC PRINCIPLES

We have considered that subject of the extent of the atonement solely in connection with the scriptural statements bearing upon this particular point,—and in connection with the views taught us generally in Scripture with regard to the nature, objects, and effects of the atonement itself,—without much more than merely incidental allusions to the connection between this and the other doctrines that are usually controverted between the Calvinists and the Arminians. We have adopted this course, because we were anxious to show that the doctrine of particular redemption,—or of an atonement limited in its destination, though not in its intrinsic sufficiency,—which is commonly reckoned the weakest part of the Calvinistic system, and seems to be regarded by many as having no foundation to rest upon except its accordance with the other doctrine of Calvinism,—is quite capable of standing upon its own proper merits,—upon its own distinct and independent evidence,—without support from the other doctrines which have been commonly held in combination with it. It is proper, however, to point out more distinctly, as a not unimportant subject of investigation,—though we can do little more than point it out,—the bearing of this doctrine upon some of the other departments of the Calvinistic or Arminian controversy.

The Arminians are accustomed to argue in this way: Christ died for all men,—that is, with a, purpose, design, or intention of saving all men; leaving it, of course, to the free will of each man individually to determine whether or not he will concur with this purpose of God, embrace the provision, and be saved. And if Christ died for all men, then it follows that there could not be any eternal decree by which some men were chosen to life, and others passed by and left to perish. Thus, upon the alleged universality of the atonement, they founded a distinct and independent argument against the Calvinistic doctrine of predestination; and this argument, as I formerly had occasion to mention, is strongly urged by Cureellæus and Limborch, and others of the ablest Arminian writers. The Calvinists meet this argument by asserting that Christ did not die for all men, but only for some, in the Sense in which I have had occasion to explain these statements; and by establishing this position on its own proper evidence, they not only refute the argument against predestination, but bring out an additional confirmation of its truth. All this is plain enough, so far as the general sequence and connection of the argument is concerned. But the question occurs, What do the Calvinistic universalists make of it? They believe that Christ died for all men, and they also believe in the eternal, absolute election of some men to salvation. Of course they are bound to maintain that these two things are consistent with each other, and on this particular point,—namely, the consistency of these two doctrines—they have both the Arminians and the great body of the Calvinists to contend against; for Calvinists, in general, have admitted that, if the Arminians could establish their position, that Christ died for all men, the conclusion of the falsehood of the Calvinistic doctrine of election could not be successfully assailed.

The way in which this matter naturally and obviously presents itself to the mind of a believer in the doctrine of election is this,—and it is fully accordant with Scripture,—that God must be conceived of as, first, desiring to save some of the lost race of men, and electing or choosing out those whom He resolved to save,—a process which Scripture uniformly ascribes to the good pleasure of His will, and to no other cause whatever; and then,—that is, according to our mode of conceiving of the subject, for there Can be no real succession of time in the infinite mind,—decreeing, as the great mean in order to the attainment of this end, and in consistency with His perfections law, and government, to send His son to seek and save them,—to suffer and die in their room and stead. The mission of His Son, and all that flowed from it, we are thus to regard as a result or consequence of God's having chosen some men to everlasting life, and thus adopting the best and wisest means of executing this decree, of carrying this purpose into effect. If this be anything like the true state of the case, then it is plain that God never had any real design or purpose to save all men,—or to save any but those who are saved; and that His design or purpose to saving the elect continued to exist and to operate during the whole process,—regulating the divine procedure throughout, and determining the end and object contemplated in sending Christ into the world, and in laying our iniquities upon Him. This view of the matter, Calvinists, in general, regard as fully sanctioned by the statements of Scripture, and as fully accordant with the dictates of right reason, exercised upon all that we learn from Scripture, or from any other source, with respect to the divine perfections and government. The course which the Calvinistic universalists usually adopt in discussing this point,—in order to show at once against the Arminians, that, notwithstanding the admitted universality of the atonement, the doctrine of election may be true, and to show, against the generality of Calvinists, that, notwithstanding the admitted doctrine of election, the universality of the atonement may be true,—is this, they try to show that we should conceive of God as first decreeing to send His Son into the world to suffer and die for all men, so as to make the salvation of all men possible, and to lay a foundation for tendering it to them all; and then, foreseeing that all men would reject this provision, if left to themselves, decreeing to give to some men, chosen from the human race in general, faith and repentance, by which their salvation might he secured.

Now, the discussion of these topics involves an investigation of some of the most difficult and abstruse questions connected with the subject of predestination; and on these we do not at present enter. We would only remark, that the substance of the answer given to these views of the Calvinistic universalists, may be embodied in these positions,—leaving out the general denial of the universality of the atonement, which is not just the precise point at present under consideration, though sufficient of itself, if established, to settle it,—First, that the general will or purpose to save all men conditionally is inconsistent with scriptural views of the divine perfections,—of the general nature and operation of the divine decrees,—and of the principles by which the actual salvation of men individually is determined; and really amounts, in substance, to a virtual, though not an intentional, betrayal of the true Calvinistic doctrine of election into the hands of its enemies. Secondly, and more particularly, that this method of disposing and arranging the order of the divine decrees,—that is, according to our mode of conceiving of them, in making the decree to send Christ to die for men, precede the decree electing certain men for whom He was to die, and whom, by dying, He was certainly to save,—is inconsistent with what Scripture indicates upon this subject. This is, indeed, in substance, just the question which used to be discussed between the Calvinists and the Arminians upon the point,—whether or not Christ is the cause and foundation of the decree of election—the Arminians maintaining that He is, and the Calvinists that He is not,—a question of some intricacy, but of considerable importance, in its bearing upon the subject of election generally, which will be found discussed and settled in Turretine,* on the decrees of God and predestination. I may also observe, that, in the last Quæstio of the same Locus,† under the head of the order of the decrees of God in predestination, there is a very masterly exposure of the attempts of Calvinistic universalists to reconcile their doctrine, in regard to the extent of the atonement, with the doctrine of election, by deviating from what Calvinists have generally regarded as the right method of arranging the order of the divine decrees,—according to our mode conceiving of them,—by representing atonement as preceding election in the divine purpose; and, what is very interesting and instructive, his arguments fully meet and dispose of all grounds taken by the best writers on the opposite side in our own day. In the portion of this Quæstio to which I more immediately refer, he is arguing, of course, with the school of Cameron and Amyraldus,—the hypothetic or conditional universalists, as they were generally called by the divines of the seventeenth century. Of the various and discordant parties composing the defenders of unlimited atonement in our own day, Dr Wardlaw is the one whose views most entirely concur with those of the founders of the school. His views, indeed, exactly coincide with theirs,—he has deviated no further from sound doctrine than they did, and not nearly so far as most of the modern defenders of an unlimited atonement. Accordingly, the statement which Turretine gives of the views and arguments of those who defended universal atonement, in combination with election, embodies the whole substance of what Dr Wardlaw has adduced in defence of his principles, in his work on the nature and extent of the atonement,—and the argument is put at least as ably and as plausibly as it has even been since; while Turretine, in examining it, has conclusively answered all that Dr Wardlaw has adduced, or that any man could adduce, to reconcile the doctrine of an unlimited atonement with the Calvinistic doctrine of election.*

I think it useful to point out such illustrations of the important truth, that almost all errors in theology,—some of them occasionally eagerly embraced as novelties or great discoveries when they happen to be revived,—were discussed and settled by the great theologians of the seventeenth century.

There is only one point in the representations and arguments of Calvinistic universalists, to which I can advert more particularly. It is the practice of describing the atonement as intended for, and applicable to, all; and representing the whole specially of the case, with reference to results, as lying, not in the atonement itself, but merely in the application which God, in His sovereignty, resolved or decreed to make, and does make, of it; and then calling upon us, with the view of giving greater plausibility to this representation, to conceive of, and to estimate, the atonement by itself, and wholly apart from its application,—or from the election of God, which, they admit, determined its application, to individuals. Now, this demand is unreasonable,—it implies misconception, and it is fitted to lead to greater misconception. Our duty, of course, is just to contemplate the atonement, as it is actually presented to us in Scripture, in all the connections and relations in which it stands. We know nothing of the atonement but what the Bible makes known to us; and, in order to know it aright, we must view it just as the Bible represents it. The scheme of salvation is a great system of purposes and actings, on the part of God, or of truth and doctrines which unfold to us these purposes and actings. The series of things, which are done and revealed with a view to the salvation of lost men, constitute a great and harmonious system,—devised, superintended, and executed by infinite wisdom and power, and complete in all its parts, which work together for the production of glorious result. And when we attempt to take this scheme to pieces, and to separate what God has joined together, we are in great danger of being left to follow our own devices, and to fall into error, especially if we do not take care to base our full and final conclusion, in regard to any one department of the scheme, upon a general survey of the whole. We admit that the atonement, viewed by itself, is just vicarious suffering, of infinite worth and value, and of course, intrinsically sufficient to expiate the sins of all men. There is on dispute about this point. This admission does not satisfy our opponents, and does not in the least incommode us. The question in dispute turns upon the destination or intended object, not the intrinsic sufficiency, of the atonement. We cannot conceive of anything intermediate between intrinsic sufficiency on the one hand, and actual or intended application on the other. The actual application of the atonement extends to those only who believe and are forgiven. And Calvinists,—although they may think it convenient, for controversial purposes, to argue for a time, as Dr wardlaw does, upon the supposition of atonement without election—must admit that this actual application of the atonement was, in each case, foreseen and fore-ordained. There could be no intended application of the atonement, contrary, or in opposition, to that which is actually made, and made because it was intended from eternity. The doctrine of the atonement may be said to consist of its intrinsic sufficiency and of its intended application. These two heads exhaust it: and when men hold up what they call the atonement, per se, viewed by itself and apart from its application, and yet will not admit that description corresponds to, and is exhausted by, its infinite intrinsic sufficiency, they must mean by this,—for there is no medium,—an intended application of the atonement different from the application that is in fact made of it, in actually pardoning and saving men. But this is manifestly not theatonement, per se, viewed by itself, and apart from its application; so that the supposition on which they are fond of arguing has really no meaning or relevancy, and tends only to perplex the subject, and to involve in doubt and obscurity the sovereign election of God in the salvation of sinners.

The truth is, that the atonement, apart from its application, actual or intended, cannot be conceived of in any other sense than with reference merely to its intrinsic sufficiency; and the question truly in dispute really amounts, in substance, to this,—whether, besides the actual application of the atonement to some men, in their actual pardon and acceptance,—which, of course, our Calvinistic opponents must admit to have been intended and fore-ordained,—there was a different intended, though never realized application of it to all men,—some design, purposes, or intention, on God's part, of saving all men through its means. And it was just because the question really turned, not upon anything we know, or can know, about the atonement viewed in itself, and apart from its application, but upon the purposes or design of God in giving His Son, and of Christ in giving Himself, for men, that the whole subject was frequently discussed, in the seventeenth century, under the head of universal grace,—that is, the universal love or kindness of God, in designing and providing, by sending His Son into the world, for the salvation of all men; and I am persuaded that it is chiefly from overlooking the consideration, that the whole question does, and must, turn upon the purposes, or design, of God and Christ in the matter, and the consequent destination of what they did,—and from getting themselves entangled in the consideration of what they call the atonement per se,—that any men who hold the doctrine of election have succeeded in persuading themselves of the universality of the atonement. The investigation of the will or decree—the purpose or design—of God, in the matter, belongs properly to the head of predestination; and under that head Calvinistic divines have fully proved that no such will, purposes, or design, to save all men, as the doctrine of universal atonement necessarily implies, can be reconciled with what is taught in Scripture, and confirmed by right reason, with respect to the divine decrees.

The history of theology affords abundant evidence of the tendency of the doctrine of universal atonement to distort and pervert men's views of the scheme of divine truth, though, of course, this tendency has been realized in very different degrees. There have been some theologians in whose minds the doctrine seemed to lie, without developing itself, to any very perceptible extent, in the production of any other error. With these persons, the doctrine, that Christ died for all men, seems to have been little or nothing more than just the particular form or phraseology in which they embodied the important truth of the warrant and obligation to preach the gospel to every creature,—to invite and require men, without distinction or exception, to come to Christ, and to embrace Him, that they might receive pardon, acceptance, and eternal life. In such cases, the error really amounts to little more than a certain inaccuracy of language, accompanied with some indistinctness or confusion of thought. Still it should not be forgotten that all error is dangerous, and that this is a point where, as experience shows, error is peculiarly apt to creep in, in subtle and insidious disguises, and to extend its ravages more widely over the field of Christian truth, than even the men who cherish it may, for a time, be themselves aware of.

The first and most direct tendency of this doctrine is to lead men to dilute and explain away—as I have illustrated at length—the scriptural statements with respect to the true nature and import of the substitution and satisfaction of Christ, and their bearing upon the redemption and reconciliation of sinners. And this introduces serious error into a most fundamental department of Christian truth. There are men, indeed, who, while holding the doctrine of universal atonement, still make a sound profession in regard to the true nature and immediate effects of Christ's death. But this is only because they do not fully comprehend their own principles, and follow them out consistently; and, of course, their tenure even of the truth they hold rests upon a very insecure foundation. But the progress of error in many cases does not stop here. The idea very naturally occurs to men, that, if Christ died for all the human race, then some provision must have been made for bringing within all men's reach, and making accessible to them, the privileges or opportunities which have been thus procured for them. And as a large portion of the human race are, undoubtedly, left in entire ignorance of Christ, and of all that He has done for them, some universalists have been led, not very unnaturally, to maintain the position,—that men may be, and that many have been, saved through Christ, or on the ground of His atonement, who never heard of Him, to whom the gospel was never made known, though Scripture surely teaches—at least in regard to adults—that their salvation is dependent upon their actually attaining to a knowledge of what Christ has done for men, and upon their being enabled to make a right use and application of the knowledge with which they are furnished. It is very easy and natural, however, to advance a step further, and to conclude that since Christ died for all men, He must have intended to remove, and have actually removed, not only some, but all, obstacles to their salvation; so that all, at least, to whom He is made known, must have it wholly in their own power to secure their salvation. And this naturally leads to a denial, or at least a dilution, of the doctrine of man's total depravity, and of the necessity of the special supernatural agency of the Spirit, in order to the production of faith and regeneration; or—what is virtually the same thing—to the maintenance of the doctrine of what is called universal sufficient grace—that is, that all men have sufficient power or ability bestowed upon them to repent and believe, if they will only use it aright.

Calvinistic universalists can, of course, go no further than universal grace in the sense of God's universal love to men, and design to save them, and universal redemption, or Christ dying for all men. The Arminians follow out these views somewhat more fully and consistently, by taking in also universal vocation, or a universal call to men,—addressed to them either through the word, or through the works of creation and providence,—to trust in Christ, or at least in God's offered mercy, accompanied, in every instance, with grace sufficient to enable them to accept of this call. In like manner, it is nothing more than a consistent and natural following out of the universal grace and universal redemption, to deny the doctrine of election, and thus to overturn the sovereignty of God in the salvation of sinners; and it is not to be wondered at, that some have gone further still, and asserted the doctrine of universal salvation,—the only doctrine that really remove any of the difficulties of this mysterious subject, though, of course, it does so at the expense of overturning the whole authority of revelation. Men have stopped at all

these various stages, and none are to be charged with holding anything
which they disclaim; but experience, and the nature of the case, make
it plain enough, that the maintenance of universal grace and universal
atonement has a tendency to lead men in the direction we have indicated;
and this consideration should impress upon us the necessity of taking
care lest we should incautiously admit views which may, indeed, seem
plausible and innocent, but which may eventually involve us in dangerous error.

I must now terminate the discussion of this whole subject, and proceed to consider the other leading doctrines involved in the controversy
between the Calvinists and the Arminians. I have dwelt longer upon
this doctrine of the atonement than upon any other. The subject is of
fundamental importance, both theoretically and practically; both in its
bearing upon a right comprehension of the scheme of Christian truth,
and upon the discharge of the duties incumbent upon us, viewed either simply as men who have souls to be saved, or as bound to seek
the salvation of others. And there is much in the present condition of
the church, and in the existing aspects of our theological literature, to
enhance the importance of thoroughly understanding this great doctrine,—having clear and definite conceptions of the principal points
involved in it,—and being familiar with the scriptural evidence on which
our convictions regarding it rest. The atonement forms the very centre
and keystone of the Christian system. It is most intimately connected,
on the one side (or a priori), with all that is revealed to us concerning
the natural state and condition of men, and concerning the nature and
character of Him who came in God's name to seek and to save them;
and, on the other hand (or a posteriori), with the whole provision made
for imparting to men individually the forgiveness of their sins,—the
acceptance of their persons,—the renovation of their natures,—and,

finally, an inheritance among them that are sanctified; and it is well fitted to guard against defective and erroneous views upon the subject of the atonement, that we should view it in its relation to the whole counsel of God, and to the whole scheme of revealed truth. The atonement is the great manifestation of God,—the grand means of accomplishing His purposes. The exposition of the true nature, causes, and consequences of the sufferings and death of the Son of God,—the unfolding of the true character, the objects, and effects, of His once offering up of Himself a sacrifice,—constitutes what is more strictly and peculiarly the gospel of the grace of God, which, according to the commandment of the everlasting God, is to be proclaimed to all nations for the obedience of faith. The only legitimate herald of the cross is the man who has been taught by God's word and Spirit to understand the true nature and application of this great provision,—who, in consequence, has been led to take his stand, for his own salvation, upon the foundation which has been laid in Zion,—and who is able also to go round about Zion, to mark her bulwarks, and to consider her palaces,—to unfold the true nature and operation of the great provision which God has made for saving sinners, by sending His own Son to suffer and die for them. And with special reference to the peculiar errors of the present time, there are two dangers to be jealously guarded against: first, the danger of attempting to make the cross of Christ more attractive to men,—to make the representations of the scheme of redemption better fitted, as we may fancy, to encourage and persuade men to come to Christ, and to trust in Him, by keeping back, or explaining away anything which God has revealed to us regarding it,—by failing to bring out, in its due order and right relations, every part of the scheme of revealed truth; and, secondly, the danger of underrating the value and the efficacy of the shedding of Christ's precious blood, of the decease which He once accomplished at Jerusalem, as if it were fitted and intended merely to remove legal obstacles, and to open a door for salvation to all, and not to effect and secure the actual salvation of an innumerable multitude,—as if it did not contain a certain provision—an effectual security—that Christ should see of the travail of His soul and be satisfied; that He should appear at length before His Father's throne, with the whole company of the ransomed,—with all whom He washed from their sins in His own blood, and made kings and priests unto God, saying, "Behold, I and the children whom Thou hast given Me!"

www.ingramcontent.com/pod-product-compliance
Lightning Source LLC
Chambersburg PA
CBHW051311120626
46547CB00015B/2180